Teaching in Further Education

The Bedford Way Papers Series

Teaching in Further Education
New perspectives for a changing context

Norman Lucas

Bedford Way Papers

INSTITUTE OF
EDUCATION
UNIVERSITY OF LONDON

For my father
D.M. Lucas

First published in 2004 by the Institute of Education, University of London,
20 Bedford Way, London WC1H 0AL
www.ioe.ac.uk

Pursuing Excellence in Education

British Library Cataloguing in Publication Data:
A catalogue record for this publication is available from the British Library

ISBN 0 85473 700 6

Design and typography by Joan Rose
Cover design by Andrew Chapman

Production services by
Book Production Consultants plc, Cambridge

Printed by Piggott Black Bear Ltd, Cambridge

Contents

Preface

Most studies in the past have focused on the practice of teachers in schools with some reference to higher education. The importance of this book is that it brings together available knowledge, literature and research on teachers in further education (FE), who teach over 6 million learners in England per year.

The last decade or so has seen fundamental changes in the management, funding and make up of learners in further education, which is now part of what is referred to by policy makers as the much broader Learning and Skills Sector. For those teaching in FE the amount of recent initiatives and upheavals can seem bewildering and seemingly contradictory. This book focuses on the practice of teachers caught within this period of change and upheaval.

This is not a 'handbook' for those learning to teach in FE. The aim of this book is to set the historical and contemporary context, which has as its central motif the professionalisation of teachers in further education. As such the book will appeal to all FE teachers as well as a wide audience across the Learning and Skills Sector who wish to get a broader perspective on teaching and learning.

This book explores different ways of understanding and conceptualising the professional development and practice of those working in FE. The book begins by locating its concern with their practice in the historical legacy and recent attempts to reform the FE sector, moving on to analyse the development of initial teacher education and professional development for FE teachers from its 'voluntarist' past to the introduction of more regulation in the form of compulsory teaching qualifications and national standards. It describes and illuminates the diversity of teaching and learning in FE and explores a number of models of practice and their application to initial teacher education and professional development programmes.

Teaching in Further Education: New perspectives for a changing context critically discusses the present context of change and regulation highlighting the contradictory pressures faced by teachers and policy makers. Finally the book proposes a radical restructuring, a new professional framework and a new agenda for rethinking the professional practice and knowledge base of FE teachers.

Abbreviations

ABSSU	Adult Basic Skills Strategy Unit
ACSETT	Advisory Committee on the Supply and Training of Teachers
AE	Adult Education
AEI	Adult Education Institute
AfC	Association for Colleges
ALF	Average Level of Funding
ALI	Adult Learning Inspectorate
AoC	Association of Colleges
APL	Accreditation of Prior Learning
APEL	Accreditation of Prior Experiential Learning
AVCE	Advanced Vocational Certificate of Education
BTEC	Business and Technology Education Council
CATE	Council for the Accreditation of Teacher Education
CATS	Credit and Accumulation Transfer System
CBET	Competence-Based Education and Training
C&G	City and Guilds London Institute
Cert. Ed	Certificate of Education
CNAA	Council for National Academic Awards
CoVES	Centres of Vocational Excellence
CPD	Continuing Professional Development
CPVE	Certificate of Pre-Vocational Education
DES	Department for Education and Science
DfE	Department for Education
DfEE	Department for Education and Employment
DfES	Department for Education and Skills
DLE	Demand Lead Element
DoE	Department of Education
DSA	Department of Science and Art
DVE	Diploma of Vocational Education
ED	Education Department
ET	Employment Training
ENTO	Employment National Training Organisation
ESOL	English for Speakers of Other Languages
FE	Further Education

FEDA	Further Education Development Agency
FEFC	Further Education Funding Council
FENTO	Further Education National Training Organisation
FESDF	Further Education Staff Development Forum
FEU	Further Education Unit
GCSE	General Certificate of Secondary Education
GEST	Grant for Educational Support and Training
GNVQ	General National Vocational Qualification
GRIST	Grant Related In-Service Training
GTC	General Teaching Council
HE	Higher Education
HEFC	Higher Education Funding Council
HEI	Higher Education Institution
HESDA	Higher Education Staff Development Agency
HMI	Her Majesty's Inspectorate
HNC	Higher National Certificate
HND	Higher National Diploma
HRD	Human Resource Development
HRM	Human Resource Management
ILT	Institute for Learning and Teaching
INSET	In-Service Education and Training
ISR	Individual Student Record
IT	Information Technology
ITB	Industrial Training Board
ITE	Initial Teacher Education
ITOs	Industry Training Organisations
IWF	Institutional Weighting Factor
JTS	Junior Technical School
LCC	London County Council
LEA	Local Education Authority
LEATGS	Local Education Authority Training Grants Scheme
LIBs	Lead Industry Bodies
LLLSSC	Lifelong Learning Sector Skills Council
LLSCs	Local Learning and Skills Councils
LMC	Local Management of Colleges
LSDA	Learning and Skills Development Agency
LSC	Learning and Skills Council
MA	Modern Apprenticeship
MCI	Management Charter Initiative

MIS	Management Information System
MoE	Ministry of Employment
MSC	Manpower Services Commission
NATFHE	National Association of Teachers in Further and Higher Education
NCVQ	National Council for Vocational Qualifications
NETTS	National Education and Training Targets
NIACE	National Institute for Adult and Community Education
NRDC	National Research and Development Centre
NTI	New Training Initiative
NTO	National Training Organisation
NTONC	National Training Organisation National Committee
NVQ	National Vocational Qualification
Ofsted	Office for Standards in Education
PAULO	National Training Organisation for Adult and Community Education and Youth Work
PCFC	Polytechnics and Colleges Funding Council
PGCE	Post Graduate Certificate in Education
PwC	PricewaterhouseCoopers
QCA	Qualifications and Curriculum Authority
QTS	Qualified Teacher Status
RDAs	Regional Development Agencies
RVQs	Review of Vocational Qualifications
SSC	Sector Skills Council
SEN	Special Educational Needs
SOEID	Scottish Office Education and Industry Department
SCOTVEC	Scottish Vocational Education Council
SSDA	Sector Skills Development Agency
SVQ	Scottish Vocational Qualifications
TDLB	Training and Development Lead Body
TEC	Training and Enterprise Council
TESOL	Teaching English as an Overseas Language
TRIST	TVEI Related In-Service Training
TOPS	Training Opportunity Scheme
TTA	Teacher Training Agency
TUC	Trade Union Congress
TVEI	Training and Vocational Education Initiative
UCET	University Council for the Education of Teachers
UfI	University for Industry
UPDC	Universities Professional Development Consortium

VET	Vocational Education and Training
YOPS	Youth Opportunities Programme
YTS	Youth Training Scheme

Part 1

FURTHER EDUCATION
IN CONTEXT

1 From technical to further education colleges

Introduction

This chapter describes and analyses changes in technical, vocational and further education (FE) from their origins in the nineteenth century, up to college incorporation in 1993 when colleges were taken away from LEA control.[1] Building upon previous work (Green and Lucas 1999) this opening chapter traces the development of FE from its early *ad hoc* beginnings to the early 1990s, analysing the development of FE through four historical phases (chapter 2 represents a fifth phase). The importance of the historical perspective is that it shows the origins of what has been described as the impoverished legacy and unplanned development of the FE sector, and the neglect of FE colleges by policy makers. Despite the advances made towards local education authorities taking responsibility for further education in the post-1944 era, technical and then FE colleges developed very unevenly in terms of the range of students, diversity of curriculum offer, and variety of professional practice on the part of FE college teachers. Alongside the growing diversity of FE colleges, during what is described as the fourth historical phase, there was increasing intervention from central government in vocational and pre-vocational programmes and a growing concern about efficiency, public accountability and effectiveness. The account of the haphazard development of further education in this chapter suggests that the legacy of the past remains a strong feature of present college provision and, together with chapters 2 and 3, frames my later examination of the professional practice of further education teachers.

The impoverished legacy

Records from the nineteenth century concerning further or vocational education are very scant and unclear (McNair Report 1944). There are difficulties in distinguishing between the terms 'adult', 'technical' and 'vocational' education. Technical education is sometimes used to mean adult vocational education and sometimes to refer to technical education in schools. The use of the word 'school' can mean what we would describe today as a college, and the use of the word 'adult' needs to be set within the context that it was only in 1899 that the school leaving age was raised to 12, and it took until 1922 to implement its rise to 14 years of age. There are some records of public debates about technical education such as those conducted by the Board of Trade in 1851 (Bristow 1970), but most were concerned with technical education in schools. By and large, however, further education was not considered or given any priority by central government until the 1944 Education Act (Barnett 1986).

Green has argued that further education has a long, though relatively hidden, history going back to developments in the later stages of the industrial revolution (Green 1990). Adult or community education in its broadest sense can be traced back beyond the nineteenth century; for example the Sheffield Societies were formed by mechanics in 1792 and were a mixture of self-education and radical political organisation (Thompson 1963). There was some adult literacy education provided by the church in the eighteenth century to enable the 'poorer classes' to read the Bible. There were also Schools of Industry after 1795, which emphasised learning trades, manual skills and the 'habits of industry' (Cotgrove 1958). Most adult education for poorer people was undertaken by mutual improvement societies (Hyland and Merrill 2003).

Nineteenth-century technical education and training in England had a number of strands. These included work-based apprenticeship, the various schools and self-improvement associations of the labour and co-operative movement, the Mechanics' Institutes, the Evening Institutes and other adult education institutions, which received philanthropic and state funding (Simon 1965).

The dominant form of technical training in England during the first half of the nineteenth century was the apprenticeship, which was organised by independent employers and craftsmen with no public funds and little public regulation (Aldrich 1999). It usually involved workplace training with little or no theoretical or academic study, and was distinct from mainstream educational provision (Ainley and Rainbird 1999). As voluntary provision made by employers without state regulation it fitted well with the dominant liberal philosophy of 'voluntarism' in education and training, and in many ways set the parameters for all further developments in post-school technical education and training (Green 1990).

The other main tradition of adult education in the early nineteenth century was that of working-class 'self-help education', often organised through small associations and clubs and, on a larger scale, through the institutions of the labour and co-operative movements (Hyland and Merrill 2003). In this tradition, adult education took a myriad different forms that were a mixture of education and radical politics, from the common reading circles of working men and women to the Owenite Halls of Science, the 'schools' organised by the Chartists, Christian Socialists, night schools and others. An example of the latter was the London Working Men's College formed in 1854 by the Christian Socialists to provide education for working men (Harrison 1954). This attracted a remarkable group of volunteer teachers such as Maurice, Ruskin, Furnival, and Rosetti (Edwards 1961). Although 'practical knowledge' was highly valued in this tradition, the emphasis tended to be on developing working-class literacy, general culture and, above all, political awareness (Thompson 1963).

The principal precursors of the late nineteenth-century technical colleges were the Mechanics' Institutes, the first of which was founded in Edinburgh in 1821 (Bristow 1970). However, it was the foundation of the London Mechanics' Institution and the famous lectures by Dr Birkbeck that led to the establishment of these institutions in other parts of the country (Cotgrove 1958). The Mechanics' Institutes did not win credibility as genuinely mass adult education providers because their major emphasis was access to scientific knowledge through the reading of tracts and pamphlets (Cotgrove 1958) and assumed a high level of literacy. The increasingly middle-class ethos of Mechanics' Institutes alienated potential working-class recruits. Furthermore, working-class initial education was often too limited to allow them to benefit from what the Institutes had to offer (Green and Lucas 1999). An example of how many working

class students failed to cope was recorded in 1857 by the Reverend
Mitchell concerning a parochial evening school in Shoreditch. He noted
that many who enrolled in evening class soon dropped out because they
found the

> drudgery of going through the rudiments very great and almost unbearable.
> With the good motive of desiring knowledge they are led to school and
> think they shall soon be able to read; but, on finding their mistake, even if
> the teacher has the power of putting information before them in an unusu-
> ally attractive way, they frequently discontinue their attendance.
>
> (Edwards 1961: 18)

In fact, the Institutes established the dubious tradition of separating general, scientific and technical education from practical craft instruction
(Evans 1975).

Common to all these strands of adult education and training was their
predominantly voluntary and part-time character. The state played a relatively minor role in apprentice training and formal technical schooling,
at least until later in the century, and was generally opposed to the tradition of radical working-class self-education (Green 1990). Michael
Sadler well encapsulated the strengths and weaknesses of the part-time,
voluntary tradition of evening classes in the nineteenth century:

> evening classes have borne the characteristic features of the English edu-
> cational organisation. Free in their development ... often well-adapted to
> the requirements of the persevering and strong ... and from the national
> point of view insufficiently adjusted to the needs of the rank and file.
>
> (quoted in Roderick and Stephens 1978: 21)

By the mid-nineteenth century, there was increasing criticism of this
voluntary tradition. Following the Great Exhibition of 1851, great concern was expressed about the state of technical education and a Department of Science and Art (DSA) was established under the Board of Trade
in 1853 to stimulate and co-ordinate efforts in technical education (Bristow 1970). The DSA had some success in the establishment of schools of
art and design, but made little impact until the next decade in establish-

ing science classes. A mere £898 was spent on science classes in the first six years, underlining the initial intention that the DSA would only provide support to an existing system which would continue to be local, voluntary and, in the main, self-supporting (Bishop 1971).

It was not until the late 1880s that a more dynamic and systematic approach was adopted in relation to the development of public technical education, in part as a response to the criticisms of the existing system made by the Samuelson Royal Commission on Technical Instruction in 1884 (Roderick and Stevens 1978). Examination boards had been established with the foundation of the Royal Society of Arts Examination Board (1856) and the City and Guilds of London Institute (1879); the latter was created by the City of London Livery Companies to give accreditation to the growing number of vocational students (Foden 1992). An important development during this period was the establishment of the London Artisans' Club in 1868. This was supported by the emerging trade union movement because of the growing demand by craftsmen to improve their training, a role for which science and art classes were unsuited (Cotgrove 1958). Following this was the establishment of the Trades Guild of Learning (1873) and the Artisans' Institute of 1874. The City and Guilds played a part in the foundation in 1883 of the Finsbury Technical College, which offered daytime and evening courses in mathematics and science and in vocational subjects such as engineering and building (Foden 1992). They also collaborated with the new Regent Street Polytechnic, opened by Quintin Hogg, which offered instruction in bricklaying, plumbing, electrical work, watch-making, printing, photography and tailoring (Cotgrove 1958).

The pattern of technical education which developed in the nineteenth century was not only institutionally marginalised from mainstream education, it was also intellectually adrift. Science also became separated from the classical curriculum.

This distinction was not apparent in the 18th century when scientific and technical studies were widely included in the curricula, especially in private academies, as part of general education. But classical education divorced from science became a sign of social privilege, and science became identified with useful knowledge, to be studied as a vocational subject, rather than as part of a liberal education.

(Cotgrove 1958: 16)[2]

While in most of the more advanced northern European countries such as France and Germany technical education was closely allied to general education, in Britain a sharp divide grew between the two, separating skills and knowledge (Day 1987). The continental system was particularly strong in preparing those who would eventually occupy higher level positions as technicians and engineers (Weiss 1982).

By comparison with the French system in the mid-nineteenth century, English technical training was a very minimalist affair (Green 1990). Its prototypical form was the employer-controlled apprenticeship whose archetypal product was the useful 'practical man' and whose main standard of quality was time served (Sheldrake and Vickerstaff 1987). Sylvanus Thompson, the first Principal of Finsbury Technical College, referred to the apprenticeship as six years of dull, repetitive drudgery that failed 'to make anything but a bad, unintelligent machine' (Thompson 1879). This may be rather harsh since, whereas with a neglectful employer the apprentice might learn very little, with a conscientious one he (rarely she) might at least get a good grounding in the basics of his trade. However, what he did not acquire, at least not through his apprenticeship, was any broader culture or much theoretical knowledge. The technical colleges later made up for the latter but not the former (Green and Lucas 1999).

The overall picture of nineteenth-century technical and vocational education is therefore one of fragmented, *ad hoc* and marginalised provision (Green 1990). This is related to the fact that, unlike in other European countries, the state in England did not initially play a direct role in fostering industrialisation either by directing capital into industry or by training in new skills. Companies were left to invest in training as they saw fit and many did not see it as a high priority (Barnett 1986). The liberal, voluntarist creed, which generally preferred voluntary initiatives to state intervention in education and training, applied particularly in the area of technical education, which was seen as a low priority for government and whose public promotion raised fears about increased taxation, loss of trade secrets, restrictions on child labour and the undermining of employer initiative. The developmental role played by the state was, therefore, correspondingly limited until the latter part of the century (Barnett 1986). Records about the quality of teaching are very scant (McNair Report 1944). There were some complaints concerning the quality of science instruction in 1868 (Cotgrove 1958) and there were complaints that 'instructors' received no training (Richardson 1939).[3]

Despite some advances towards the end of the century, nineteenth-century technical education in England thus left a distinctly impoverished legacy. It was overwhelmingly part-time, intellectually narrow and it never acquired a status comparable with that achieved in certain other continental countries (Green 1990). Its form became characterised by what has been described elsewhere as an historical absence – the lack of any legitimated notion of general culture and general education within which to frame technical skills (Green and Lucas 1999). Further education would find it hard to break out of this mould and to rectify this absence.

From 1889 to 1944: marginalised provision, crisis and drift

Following the Technical Instruction Act of 1889, public funding for technical education became available, although the teaching of trade and craft processes was expressly excluded, thereby continuing the distinctions first made by the Mechanics' Institutes. Technical instruction was defined as instruction in the principles of Art and Science applicable to industries (Edwards 1961). The 1890 Local Taxation Act provided public funding for technical education and this led to the creation of a range of technical colleges and polytechnics in the 1890s which laid the foundations of the twentieth-century technical college system. These buildings became known as 'whisky-money buildings' after the 1890 Act because the duty raised on beer and spirits was passed to local authorities to fund technical education: as Sydney Webb put it, 'distilling enlightenment out of whisky and beer' (quoted in Ainley and Bailey 1997). This was a 'late outbreak of good sense' (Green 1990); it continued the tradition of the Mechanics' Institutes but excluded the teaching of trade and craft processes and established a link between local authorities and colleges that was not broken until incorporation in 1993. However, in many ways it came too late to alter the patterns which had already been established (Green and Lucas 1999).

In the 1902 Education Act (Balfour Act) the basis was laid for the expansion of post-primary and secondary education which, combined with the economic growth of the late nineteenth century, should have provided the basis for growth in technical and further education. This was to be only partially the case (Bristow 1970). Further education did expand, particularly in the commercial fields, whose popularity grew in line with the growing army of clerks servicing Britain's imperial expansion in the pre-First World War period. However, the school sector, and especially the growth of state grammar schools, continued to receive higher priority than technical colleges, and all areas of education were squeezed in the expenditure cuts in the inter-war era (Kitchen 1944). The 1902 Act did provide for some expansion of the evening continuation schools (later called Evening Institutes). More importantly, it led to the establishment of senior and junior technical schools (JTS); the latter were designed to fill the gap between the school leaving age and the age when it was possible to begin an apprenticeship. These JTSs, as they came to be known, were organised alongside senior technical schools and technical colleges and often ran their own evening classes. They were never numerous but in time some developed into technical and further education colleges (Bristow 1970). There are some records of the difficulty those schools faced getting teachers during this period[4] (LCC 1903) and there is evidence that unimaginative teaching, combined with the problems of learning after working long hours, led to poor attainment and low levels of retention (Edwards 1961).

With the end of the First World War and the rhetoric of creating a 'land fit for heroes' came the 1918 Fisher Act. This required all Local Education Authorities to provide free and obligatory day continuation schooling for those leaving school at 14 (Bailey 1990). The intention was to make attendance at Day Continuation Schools for one day a week compulsory between the ages of 14 and 18, but this proposal was lost as soon as amendments to the Act made attendance voluntary (Ferguson and Abbott 1935). There were frequent complaints that industry did not support day-release education and most students had to continue their education in evening classes (Edwards 1961). The combination of a tradition of voluntarism, the economic depression and public expenditure cuts after 1926 ensured that only one authority (Rugby) met the requirements of the Fisher Act, although a few continuation schools were established (Frankel and Reeves 1996).

According to the Principal of the Rugby Day Continuation school:

> one of the major causes of failure of the Act was the piecemeal manner in which its provisions were to come into operation, because children who lived in an area where compulsory attendance was required were at a disadvantage in competing for employment with those in a neighbouring area where the Act was not yet in force. The introduction of the Act was followed by a period of industrial depression and unrest quite unfavourable to a great educational experiment.
>
> (Richardson 1939: 62)

Junior technical schools providing post-elementary vocational education did continue to expand, with enrolments reaching around 30,000 students in 1937, but they did not develop into a comprehensive national system, and no more achieved parity of status with academic secondary schooling than did the secondary technical schools which followed the 1944 Butler Act (Bailey 1990; McCullough 1987). During this period, there was also some development of adult non-vocational education. Henry Morris pioneered community education in Cambridgeshire in the 1920s and 1930s and the Women's Institutes were founded in 1924, some years after the inauguration of the Workers Education Association in 1903. All of these developments added to the richly diverse landscape of post-school education, but fell far short of creating a national further education system (Green and Lucas 1999a).

The failure to establish the day continuation schools meant that by the 1930s most further education had reverted to its pre-war pattern and remained predominately a system of evening classes, mainly vocational in character. Edwards (1961) argues that day continuation schools would have helped technical education to escape from this confined system by beginning the transfer of work from evening classes to daytime attendance (a development anxiously awaited from 1904 onwards):

> The new schools would have solved the intractable problem of the junior evening institutes; they would have persuaded both employers and workpeople that technical education is not inevitably a matter of evening classes for the ambitious student; courses could have been transferred from scattered evening classes to day technical schools properly equipped for the purpose; technical schools relieved of the overwhelming load of junior work, would have been reorganised for advanced work built upon the solid preparation of the secondary schools and day continuation schools.
>
> (Edwards 1961: 93)

By 1937/8, only one in five children leaving elementary school at age 14 went on to any kind of further full-time education; the rest went straight into the job market. Of the 3.3 million 14–18-year-olds in England and Wales who were receiving no full-time education in 1937/8, one in 25 were on part-time courses and one in 123 in voluntary day continuation schools (Barnett 1986). Of the 80,000 pupils in 1937 who began secondary school, one in 12 ended up with the Higher School Certificate, a sixth went to some form of further education and one in 20 went to university. Most people went into the job market with no training (Barnett 1986). The attitudes of employers to training reflected the suspicion towards further education, established in the previous century, that practice is best learned in the workplace and that theoretical learning for young people resulted in them being less adaptable to 'the rough and tumble of industry and to understand more fundamentally the outlook of workmen' (Richardson 1939: 473).

The 1940s to the 1970s: technical colleges, day release and local expansion

The educational debates in the inter-war years had been dominated by the need to reform secondary education and raise the school leaving age. The war years saw a large increase in training programmes in colleges. There were 6,000 state bursaries for two-year technical degree courses; more than 4,000 students in technical colleges following six-month Higher National Certificates courses serving both industry and the armed forces; and nearly 4,000 Engineering Cadetships (Davis 1990). However, some interesting debates on post-school arrangements were aired during the war, stimulated by the publication of the Education White Paper of 1943 (Argles 1964). The John Lewis Partnership, a large retail chain, advocated a day-release for one year for all employees to study in a Technical College. The Building Apprentices and Training Council wanted compulsory technical education for apprentices up to the age of 18 (Dawn 1995). MPs and ministers also spoke of the importance of expanding technical education because of the need to rebuild and establish industry in the post-war period. There was further rapid growth after the Second World War as troops returned home and needed training for civilian life. Alongside the technical colleges, adult education institutes were established to cater for part-time academic, vocational and leisure activities (Peters 1977). Regional Advisory Councils and a National Advisory Council on Education and Industry were established and some National Colleges were set up, reflecting the growing interest amongst employers.

In the event, much of the debate was futuristic and the role of further education was squeezed out by other issues (Bristow 1970). However, the birth of further education as we know it took place in the form of a term introduced in the Education Bill of 1944, to describe what would follow the new notion of secondary education. The 'humble little clause' (41) said: 'it shall be the duty of every local education authority to secure the provision of adequate facilities for further education' (Dawn 1995: 9). It was as a result of clause 41 that it became possible for local government to build the present FE system. Although the clause was very important, the term 'further education' was only introduced following the new notion of secondary education, indicating the continuation of the marginal nature of the technical and FE colleges in comparison to the emphasis given to schools.

The 1944 Education Act sought to achieve for further education what the Fisher Act had failed to achieve with its largely un-implemented day continuation schools policy (Dawn 1995). The new Act was the first to make it a legal duty for LEAs to provide further education. Although no specific timetable was set, LEAs were required to establish and maintain county colleges, which provided school leavers with vocational, physical and practical training, thus reinforcing the vocational tradition of technical colleges. In the first year after the Act nothing extra was spent on colleges, and over the next six years the total spent was half of that spent on school medical care and nursery schools (Barnett 1986). With the election of a Labour Government in 1945 the growth of FE increased dramatically. By 1947 there were 680 establishments, double the number in 1938. Full-time students increased by some 130 per cent and the number of part-time students trebled during the same period (MoE 1946). This increased demand put pressure on the supply of teaching staff and on finding suitable accommodation (Cripps 2002). Employers were asked by Government to associate and co-operate with the new colleges and this approach led to the growing occupational training role of 'technical colleges', which gradually became institutions for 'day-release' vocational education of those in employment or those serving apprenticeships (Spours and Lucas 1996).

In 1956, a new urgency became manifest with the publication of a White Paper on Technical Education that announced legislation for further and higher education (MoE 1956). The White Paper's rationale made a direct link between these sectors and the growth of the economy, and called for increased work in higher technological and advanced technical education. It proposed a new Diploma in Technology leading to postgraduate studies. It set targets to double the number of day-release students in five years from the 335,000 there were in 1954. These targets were not met; even ten years later the number on day-release had only risen to about 650,000 (Bratchell 1968). In 1959 the Crowther Report identified FE as a crucial sector for generating economic growth but criticised it for its confusion and proliferation of courses, high part-time attendance and low retention rates, calling for more day-release and sandwich courses (CACE 1959).

The White Paper of 1961 entitled *Better Opportunities in Technical Education* put a greater emphasis on the training of technicians, craftsman and operatives (MoE 1961). By 1960 the numbers in these categories had risen to 283,000 on part-time or block-release courses, 152,000 on evening only courses, and 14,000 on full-time courses. Between 1959 and 1965/6, there was a significant shift towards full-time, sandwich and day-releases courses (Bratchell 1968) as colleges became responsive to government initiatives; the highest point of links established with local industry and employment was reached in the late 1960s to early 1970s (Spours and Lucas 1996). Selby-Smith (1970) shows how in one college in 1937/8, 78 per cent of its students were part-time, 3.8 per cent were on day-release, and 17.3 per cent were full-time. By 1964/5, the proportions had changed to 40 per cent part-time, 50.2 per cent day-release and 9.4 per cent full-time.

Throughout this period, apprenticeship remained the main vehicle of vocational training and was usually completed without any parallel off-the-job general or technical education (Summerfield and Evans 1990). For all its strengths as a means of imparting job-specific vocational skills, the apprenticeship system was being questioned as an adequate vehicle for meeting the skills needs of the economy (Sheldrake and Vickerstaff 1987). The craft unions tended to see the apprentice system as a means by which they could protect their skill status and differentials through restricting entry into tightly demarcated trades. Employers often valued the system as a way of gaining cheap labour in the absence of statutory obligations to provide training to given standards (Rainbird 1990). Both sides of industry agreed on limiting the number of apprentices, which resulted in repeated skills shortage crises not only before and during the world wars, but also increasingly during the expansionary post-1945 period (Barnett 1986).

Not only did the apprentice system provide an inadequate supply of skilled workers but it was deficient in many other ways, as the 1958 Carr Report made plain (Perry 1976). It involved unduly lengthy periods of time-serving, failed to train to any specified standards,[5] was overly narrow in the skills it imparted, and impoverished in terms of general education and theory; most damagingly, it ignored the training needs of semi-skilled workers and severely limited access to many groups, most notably women (Sheldrake and Vickerstaff 1987). As Lipshitz notes in her study of craft apprentice students, most of those released by employers to the technical colleges were boys:[6]

> The problem for girls is intensified because fewer of them get job opportunities for any type of training, especially through part-time day release. ... They have greater problems convincing employers that they are worth training at all because women are considered as having a shorter working life then men, and in effect not many courses of skilled training are open to them.
>
> (Lipshitz 1972: 2)

According to Gleeson and Mardle (1980), an important role of technical colleges during this period was to fulfil the requirements of employers and prepare apprentices or trainees to fit in with the existing occupational structures and cultures, including the division of labour based upon gender. Any questioning of the dominant assumptions was not tolerated either by technical teachers or college administrators, although some 'ex-industrial workers' were criticised for a 'lack of a professional attitude towards education' and for acting more like representatives of industry than teachers' (Venables 1967: 130). This reflected the legacy of policy makers, employers and teachers in technical colleges, who saw industrial or subject expertise as a sufficient qualification to teach (see chapter 4). Concern was expressed that newer ideas on teaching and learning did not penetrate many departments in technical colleges (Tipton 1973) and that teaching remained 'pedestrian and uninspiring' (Bristow 1970).[7]

Reflecting the 1945 Ince Report, which called for the creation of a national training scheme (Ainley and Corney 1990), numerous reports, including the government's own 1956 White Paper on technical education (MoE 1956) pointed to the relative deficiencies of British training. However, no government action was forthcoming. In 1952, the Ministry of Labour and National Service was still upholding the traditional government line that 'employers bear the major responsibility for the training of their own employees' (Sheldrake and Vickerstaff 1987: 27). The *laissez-faire* era in British training policy thus continued until the beginning of the 1960s, when renewed skills shortages, the challenge of Soviet technology, and the bulging youth cohort finally convinced government that policies on vocational training had to change (Barnett 1986).

The 1964 Industrial Training Act inaugurated the tripartite Industrial Training Boards (ITBs) to promote and co-ordinate training in the different sectors, and empowered them to redistribute the costs of training between employers by means of the levy-grant system (Senker 1992). Organised by industrial sectors but without achieving full coverage, this was never quite a national apprenticeship system, and still less a national training system for all grades of employees. However, as is suggested elsewhere, it was as near as Britain had ever come to this in its history (Green and Lucas 1999). During the brief ten years this system was in operation the volume of training did marginally increase (up by 15 per cent in those areas of manufacturing covered by the ITBs between 1964 and 1969) and notable advances were made in improving the quality of training (Sheldrake and Vickerstaff 1987). Day-release became common in many apprentice schemes; group training schemes proliferated, helping smaller firms to participate in formal training programmes; and the engineering ITB's modular training systems paved the way for greater flexibility and breadth in apprentice training (Perry 1976). However, the system was far from achieving its objectives because the quantitative gains in training provision were limited to certain skilled areas and were, in any case, soon wiped out by the decline in apprentice places which followed the onset of the recession in 1973 (Raggatt and Williams 1999). The ITBs failed to open up access to apprenticeships for previously excluded groups and did little to change the old practices of time-serving and age entry restrictions. Most seriously, little headway was made in the setting and monitoring of standards in training (Senker 1992).

It has been suggested (Ainley and Corney 1990) that the shortcomings in the practice of apprenticeships and the failure to raise standards in training showed that a national training system could not be created on the basis of devolved sectoral organisation, and that the social partners in the different sectors could not be induced to act in a co-ordinated way to create a national system of training to standards without a strong central body to co-ordinate them. Unlike in Germany, Britain's national federations and organisations for employers and unions (including the Confederation of British Industry and the Trades Union Congress) lacked binding powers over their members, and local Chambers of Commerce never attained great influence. The Central Training Council, as the TUC frequently complained, never had adequate powers to compensate for this and to ensure that the system fulfilled its objectives in meeting those long-term skills needs of the national economy which individual employers were always disposed to ignore (Perry 1976; Ainley and Corney 1990).

Despite the advances of the post-war years, what emerged was a highly uneven provision that varied substantially from one locality to another. Legislation had been permissive, not mandatory, and allowed LEAs wide scope for interpretation. Vocational education and training remained low in status and apprenticeships were dominated by the engineering and construction industries which, by the 1970s, were in decline along with other traditional industries such as ship-building and heavy engineering (Gorringe 1996). During the late 1960s and early 1970s, the economic and work-based role of technical colleges declined. As a consequence, technical colleges began to transform themselves into colleges of further education, providing a wider range of academic, vocational and pre-vocational courses. In the process they began to acquire a multi-purpose educational function (Tipton 1973).

The 1970s and 1980s: the growth of general further education colleges

Throughout the late 1970s and 1980s, full-time participation in further education rose steadily and colleges were required to respond to the needs of new types of learners including, notably, adults and school leavers who previously would have directly entered the labour market. Colleges increasingly saw themselves as 'responsive' institutions that not only served the needs of local employers but also the needs of individuals in the wider community, catering for a more diverse student population and with a mission of offering a second chance to 16–19-year-olds and adults to learn and achieve (Spours and Lucas 1996). This coincided with a period when more interest was shown in the initial training and professional development of FE college teachers and the proportion of teachers who were teacher-trained gradually rose (Cantor and Roberts 1986; Foden 1992).[8] During this period, there was a shift from the typical technical college focus on vocational day-release and evening study to the far more complex offer of the new style further education college with its increased load of full-time students following a variety of general education, vocational, general vocational and higher education courses (Hall 1994). Within the transformation of technical colleges into colleges of further education, two trends had particular influence.

First, there was the growth of academic courses for both adults and young people who wished to have a chance at achieving O and A levels (Ainley and Bailey 1997). This growth was stimulated by the expansion of higher education, which was now becoming accessible to some of those who would previously have been excluded, and by the difficulty that many schools found in maintaining viable sixth forms in the face of the falling numbers of 16–19-year-olds. Many LEAs attempted to encourage links between schools and sixth forms by establishing consortia or sixth-form centres in order to offer a reasonable range of academic courses and maintain reasonable class sizes (Green and Lucas 1999). Other LEAs removed sixth forms from schools and merged them into sixth-form colleges, or combined sixth forms with FE colleges to form tertiary colleges that provided both academic and vocational courses. Some tertiary colleges included adult education, while some LEAs maintained separate adult provision (Spours and Lucas 1996).

The second important and related factor was the decline in youth employment from the mid-1970s (Gleeson 1990). The government, in reaction to the rise in youth unemployment, took important initiatives by developing schemes for the unemployed school leaver (Avis 1987) such as the Youth Opportunities Programme (YOPS) and later, the Youth Training Scheme (YTS). For unemployed adults there was the Training Opportunity Scheme (TOPS) and, later, Employment Training (ET) (Raggatt and Williams 1999). These government initiatives reduced the levels of young people registered as unemployed, and some young people did find employment through the schemes. On the whole, however, most young people failed to find employment as a result of these schemes, although the extent of this varied from region to region depending upon the local employment opportunities (Unwin 1997).

During the mid-1980s there was a growing realisation that the disappearance of the youth labour market was not a temporary phenomenon, and this was linked to reports that stressed the importance of increasing the knowledge and skills of the workforce for changes in economic production (Gleeson 1996). Unfavourable comparisons with participation rates and education levels in other countries were made, and some reforms of the post-16 curriculum took place, expressed in proposals for a national qualifications framework (DES/ED 1991; CBI 1989). These developments in general vocational education were directly funded from central government bodies and created the mechanism for more national regulation over assessment and quality assurance. With the later development of GNVQs and NVQs there was also a greater national regulation over awarding bodies (Ecclestone 2000).

However, despite all these new initiatives and growing regulation from central government, the institutional structures of post-16 education and training were not fundamentally changed, and England and Wales continued to have a mixed system of academic and vocational courses offered by a variety of different institutions with considerable competition in the education and training market place (Hodkinson 1998). Although FE colleges were increasingly becoming a major provider of full-time 16–18 education, they failed to match the status of secondary schools because of the prestige attached to sixth forms, which remained the preferred option of many parents (Green and Lucas 1999a). Where tertiary colleges were established, and in the rare cases where they became the sole 16–19 provider in an area, a new institutional model could be seen to exist in embryonic form (Reeves 1995). Further education colleges and most tertiary colleges continued to be an awkward mixture of 16–19 and adult provision. These mixed-purpose institutions continued to form part of a complex institutional patchwork of post-16 provision which included sixth forms, sixth-form colleges and training providers, all of which came under different statutory regulations and state bodies. This patchwork of 16–19 provision was addressed in 1979 by the Macfarlane Report (DES 1979), which recommended what amounted to a new national structure of 16–19 tertiary colleges. However, the report was at odds with the government's educational agenda, and the chance to reform the system and produce an institutional structure that would be more simple, coherent and transparent disappeared amidst the vagaries of electoral politics (Green and Lucas 1999).

As organisations, colleges were often rather loose conglomerations of departments with little overall cohesion. They reflected social divisions between 'graduate and non-graduates, industrially experienced and non-experienced, craftsmen, white-collar workers, managers scientists, social scientists' (Tipton 1973: ix). This made it hard to identify colleges as a distinct type of organisation (Cavanagh and Lancaster 1983). Similarly, it was hard to identify FE college teachers as a distinct part of the teaching profession (Robson 1998). They tended to be teachers associated with particular, often competing, subject or vocational departments (Gleeson and Mardle 1980). Furthermore, departments would often follow different traditions and had different views concerning teaching and learning (Young and Lucas 1999).

FE colleges during the 1980s were extremely diverse in character and levels of resourcing. They reflected the priorities of their respective LEAs and the different communities and labour markets they served. They also reflected the diversity of policies of the different government departments, such as the Department of Employment and the Department of Education, and the agencies and awarding bodies to which they were accountable. There was no obligation on FE teachers to gain an initial teaching qualification and there was no minimum entry qualification for those seeking to teach in FE colleges (see chapter 4). The effect of the growth of FE in the 1980s was to produce a sector which had experienced 'expansion without strategic leadership' (Green 1995). However, by the end of the 1980s the issue of corporate identity and strategic planning was beginning to be discussed. The government commissioned reports from the mid-1980s, such as *Managing Colleges Efficiently* (DES 1985) or the Audit Commission's (1985) *Obtaining Better Value from Further Education*, which noted the inefficient use of resources, poorly utilised space and enviably small class sizes in many colleges. Both reports argued persuasively for greater consistency and efficiency in the use of resources. It was hard at this time to argue that FE formed a sector in any real national sense.

During this period of expansion and change, FE colleges failed to achieve the status of schools or the prestigious autonomy of universities; nor did they have a formalised relationship with employers (Hall 1994). The previous 'technical phase' of FE, related to the post-war expansion of the economy and the development of apprenticeships, had been relatively short-lived, and confined to the period of the 1950s and 1960s (Spours and Lucas 1996). Vocational education and training in England was not institutionalised in the same way as in other European systems where specialised vocational institutions were closely tied to vocational qualifications and the labour market (Green 1995). The English approach to vocational education, even at the height of its close relationship with the economy after the Second World War, always reflected its inferior status and lack of national coherence (Matlay 1997). By the late 1960s only a small proportion of 16–19-year-olds were involved in full- or part-time education and training and the majority of young people in work did not receive any form of further education and training (Pring 1995).

By the end of the 1980s, FE colleges had acquired a much more diverse mission than hitherto and were far more varied then schools, universities or polytechnics. In addition to their traditional – and still primary – focus on vocational education and training, they were now also responsible for some 40 per cent of post-16 general education courses.

However, in comparison with school sixth forms and sixth-form and tertiary colleges, they tended to accrue a disproportionate share of more disadvantaged students and those seeking a 'second chance' after unsatisfactory previous experiences of learning (Spours and Lucas 1996). Furthermore, the diversity of learners in FE colleges during the 1970s and 1980s took on a new dimension as 'new vocationalism' or 'pre-vocational' programmes were developed to offer a range of courses which emphasised preparation for work in general rather than for specific jobs (Pring 1992, 1995). As Bloomer (1997) argues, these new vocationally focused courses fuelled a debate that is still going on about their purpose and content, reflecting a growing recognition that vocational education is complex and far more than just training for job-specific skills.

As FE colleges entered the 1990s, they were both locally and nationally funded and approximately 20 per cent of their budgets consisted of targeted funding from central government departments and national government bodies (Ainley and Corney 1990).[9] Alongside this targeted funding, more regulation had also been introduced, which increased the 'influence of factors usually associated with the market, including performance indicators, accountability and vocationalism which have all been key features of the FE sector since the 1980s' (Elliott and Hall 1996: 6).

Local funding levels for FE colleges were very uneven and reflected local political decisions (Audit Commission/OFSTED 1993). Furthermore, pressure for cuts in public expenditure and the introduction of Local Management of Colleges (LMCs)[10] following the 1988 Education Act, which gave college governing bodies more power, were creating very real tensions between colleges and their LEAs. The division and rivalry between the Department of Employment and Department of Education also perpetuated further education's ambivalent position in local and national priorities, as they felt squeezed between schools, higher education and the TECs (Green and Lucas 1999a).

Conclusion

This chapter has analysed changes in technical and FE colleges from their early *ad hoc* and impoverished beginnings in the nineteenth century. Despite some advances towards the end of the nineteenth century, the system of technical education that emerged was one of part-time provision with the state playing a minor role. Technical education in England, unlike some continental states, was characterised by an absence of general education or theoretical learning within which to frame technical skills. This feature of technical education in England continued into the next century.

The chapter traced the development of technical colleges through the early twentieth century, suggesting that despite the advances made in the post-1944 era, when local education authorities took responsibility, FE colleges developed in a very uneven and haphazard way. By the 1980s, FE colleges emerged as extremely diverse in character, reflecting the different priorities of LEAs, labour markets and government departments, to which they were increasingly accountable. This produced a sector that failed to achieve the status of schools and universities, or to have a formalised relationship with employers.

By the late 1980s FE colleges had acquired a much more diverse mission than their traditional focus on vocational education and training which characterised their beginning and post-1944 development. An analysis of how FE colleges developed following incorporation in 1993 is the focus of the next chapter.

Notes

1   The incorporation of FE colleges is analysed in chapter 2.
2   Cotgrove goes on to outline how the study of Science declined at Oxford and Cambridge universities in the late nineteenth century. He argues that educational provision was linked to the class structure and church.
3   The quality and training of teachers during this period is discussed in more detail in chapter 4.
4   Edwards (1961) suggests that the only way of obtaining teachers was to recruit the best students who had taken the course.
5   The application of standards to vocational education and training is discussed in more detail in chapter 9.

6 In a study of day-release students in Scotland (Weir 1971) the only female students were those on catering courses.

7 See chapter 4.

8 This was the time of the Haycocks Reports, analysed in chapter 4.

9 Chapter 2 argues that there was a growing tendency towards regulation in the 1980s, which laid the ground for the incorporation of colleges in 1993.

10 LMC shifted the existing balance of power away from LEAs. It established a new funding formula, changed the composition of governing bodies towards more employer representatives and gave governing bodies more control over their own budgets.

2 Incorporation 1993–1999: diversity, competition and regulation

Chapter 1 focused on the somewhat haphazard development of further education from the nineteenth century to the early 1990s, analysing the development of FE through four historical phases. The focus of this chapter is on the period of the incorporation between 1993 and 1999, which can be seen as representing a fifth phase in the development.

Although the 1988 Education Reform Act altered the relationship between LEAs and colleges quite profoundly, no clear strategic leadership was provided by government departments or their national agencies. Prior to the Further and Higher Education Act 1992, further education was funded by a mixture of local rates raised by the local authority and national funding from central government raised through general taxes (Cantor *et al.* 1995). No national funding formulae existed (Birch *et al.* 1990); college funding allocations were all retrospectively calculated on the previous year's student numbers converted into full-time equivalents (FTEs) (Bradley 2000). Central government used advisory formulae as part of its assessment of need, arriving at the Standard Spending Assessments, which underpinned the Revenue Support Grant to local authorities.

As a consequence of these arrangements the detail and level of funding varied dramatically from one local authority to another (Birch *et al.* 1987), reflecting different models and calculations and the complicated funding formulae used by local government (Cantor and Roberts 1986). One difficulty in defining what FE colleges actually provided prior to incorporation was that they remained essentially local providers exhibiting diversity and variety (Scott 1995). At the time of the incorporation of colleges in 1993, staff development programmes were funded through the DfEE's Grant for Educational Support and Training (GEST) budget, which, in turn, was overseen by LEAs. However, as Huddleston and Unwin (1997) have argued, staff development in the FE college sector always had a 'mixed history' with significant variations in philosophy and approach from one LEA to another.[1] Furthermore, attitudes towards teaching qualifications varied enormously throughout the further education college sector and were rarely subject to any systematic monitoring (Guile and Lucas 1996).

In some areas, LEAs were able to influence attitudes to the professional development of FE college teachers, or chose to influence colleges to ensure that minority groups had a place in the college plan and that colleges had links with local industry and were responsive to community needs (Spours and Lucas 1996). Many colleges had good working relationships with their LEAs, but there is also evidence of some very poor ones (Graham 1997). However, on the whole, minimal quality control took place; in some cases LEAs expressed concern following a poor inspection report, but this would be retrospective and rarely had any profound implications. Atkinson (1995) argues that prior to college incorporation LEAs had some influence on priorities, but change in FE colleges was at best rather slow and long-term, with funding of colleges based on enrolments rather than achievement or retention (Bradley 1996). While this provided security and continuity for the staff, the relationship between colleges and LEAs was not conducive to rapid change. Even within the context of public expenditure savings forced on local government by successive Conservative governments in the late 1980s, there was little change in the culture and values of FE colleges.

One political aim of central government during the late 1980s and early 1990s was to undermine the power and influence of LEAs. This aim was underpinned by a belief that the introduction of markets and competition would improve provision (Smithers and Robinson 1993). Incorporation came about in the political climate of a government in its third term of office determined to give schools and colleges greater independence from LEAs and to introduce competition between providers, while at the same time giving a greater emphasis to national regulation and public accountability (FEFC 1992a). The incorporation of FE colleges was a result of the Further and Higher Education Act 1992. It removed FE and sixth-form colleges from local education authority control and changed the composition of governing bodies. For the first time FE colleges were funded centrally through the Further Education Funding Council; they became independent self-governing corporations with responsibility for their own staff, budget, assets, course planning and marketing. College corporations gained charitable status and were empowered to enter into commercial markets in order to borrow and invest funds as long as it was 'incidental' or linked to the provision of further education (see Ainley and Bailey 1997). The creation of a non-university, higher education polytechnic sector under the Polytechnics and Colleges Funding Council (PCFC) served as an example to the government that efficiency gains could be achieved by incorporated institutions when they were freed from local authorities and competed for funds (Hall 1994). For Randle and Bradey (1997), this was all part of the swing towards 'New Managerialism' which emerged in the 1980s and spread throughout the public sector.

It has also been argued that incorporation was a timely and pragmatic solution to reduce the burden of the poll tax, which the government had so badly miscalculated. So, as well as serving a political agenda, removing FE colleges from LEA control was an easy solution to bringing the poll tax levels down to the government's predicted targets. Furthermore, it has been suggested that the inclusion of sixth-form colleges in the incorporated sector was needed by the government to make up the poll tax miscalculation (Ainley and Bailey 1997). As a result of the 1992 Further and Higher Education Act, sixth-form colleges found that they were incorporated as private limited companies into the FE sector, making it more diverse than ever before.

Alongside the government's political agenda to introduce competition and undermine the power of LEAs, the form incorporation took and the methodology adopted by the FEFC was particularly influenced by three publications. The first was *Obtaining Better Value from FE* (Audit Commission 1985). This report examined the resource efficiency of 161 FE colleges and found non-viable class sizes, high drop-out rates, over-teaching and excess teaching capacity (Holloway 1999). It called upon colleges to address staff–student ratios, improve financial management and tighten up on non-teaching costs such as purchasing arrangements and cleaning.[2] In 1989 the Further Education Unit (FEU) claimed that this report brought about significant changes in the philosophy of management in FE colleges (FEU 1989).

The second important strategic document, which signalled the direction for FE in the 1990s, was the White Paper *Education and Training for the 21st Century* (DES/ED 1991). It placed FE colleges, for the first time, at the centre of a strategy for achieving higher levels of skills and qualifications. The main objectives of the White Paper were to raise levels of participation and achievement, to create a more integrated FE college sector and to make FE colleges more dynamic and efficient by placing them in a competitive market situation, encouraging them to adopt management practices from the private sector (Newman and Clark 1994).

The third important influence was the seminal report *Unfinished Business* (Audit Commission/Ofsted 1993). This report was concerned with 16–19-year-olds across the school and FE college sectors. Its major findings were that of poor student retention, poor success rates for A levels and vocational courses, and a wide variation in costs per student between institutions. It reported that an average of 12 per cent of A-level students left courses before completion and 20 per cent failed the examination. Students on vocational courses did worse with 18 per cent leaving early and 20 per cent failing the examination. The report also noted that annual revenue costs per student on courses involving three A levels, BTEC National Certificates and Diplomas varied between colleges and schools from just over £1,000 to almost £7,000 per student following the same course. Furthermore, no link was found between the cost of courses per student and subsequent examination results achieved. The report concluded that typically between 30 and 40 per cent of 16–19-year-olds who started a course did not succeed 'at a cost of £500 million – as well as a substantial waste of students' time' (Audit Commission/Ofsted 1993: 2).

The FEFC proposed that the legacy of uneven historical funding that *Unfinished Business* highlighted was to be resolved by introducing a process of 'convergence' in which the average level of funding (ALF) of each college was designed to converge by 1996/7 to plus/minus 10 per cent of the median. For many colleges, particularly those in inner cities, convergence meant coming down from previously high ALF levels (FEFC 1992). This was to be brought about by the rapid expansion of student numbers at a lower rate (FEFC 1992a). If colleges had problems with meeting their targets, there were two options: either lower the targets and extend the timescale of convergence, or start to close or merge with other colleges. During the first few years following the 1992 Act, no colleges closed, although many got into financial difficulties, seeking amalgamation and merger as a means of survival.

Atkinson (1995) argues that while the funding methodology introduced a number of new concepts, only two are key and both are linked to the findings of the three reports referenced above. First, the currency of the new FEFC system was the 'unit of activity' (or simply the 'unit'), which replaced the student full-time equivalent as the basis of calculating the amount colleges should receive.[3] The 'unit' was to be used to allow the funding to follow student learning so that if a student left the programme early the funding would also cease. The second key principle was the concept of unit funding based upon a three-stage process – 'Entry', 'On-programme' and 'Achievement' (FEFC 1992).[4] The bulk of units were allocated through the 'On-programme' element, with relatively small amounts for 'Entry' and 'Achievement'. Additional units could be earned from fee remission, childcare and additional learning support.[5] Furthermore, different quantities of units were awarded according to the type of course students followed, with 'load banding' reflecting 'cost weighting factors' according to the different resource needs of programmes. The actual amount of funding attached to achievement was small. For example, of the units linked to entry, on-programme and achievement, only 8 per cent of the total funding units was attached to achievement. As far as resources allocated to staff development were concerned, GEST funding disappeared. The new FEFC offered no advice on staff development; it merely allocated one-line budgets for colleges, leaving the allocation of funds towards staff development an individual college decision.

The basic purpose of the form incorporation took was to make colleges focus on recruitment, growth, and student retention (Drodge and Cooper

1997). The aim was to create a sector with a higher national profile and more standardised funding methods and levels so that it could be judged by national criteria for efficiency and effectiveness. The rationale for the change was to direct funds to support student learning and put pressure on colleges to focus on improving retention rates. The FEFC approach to achieving growth and improving efficiency was to base college funding on 90 per cent of the college's previous year's budget (Atkinson 1995). This was described as 'core funding'. The other 10 per cent, described as 'marginal funding', was unit-based and tied to student growth targets. However, the value of the unit within marginal funding was based upon a national average funding level. Therefore, colleges with high ALFs had to increase their student numbers, calculated in units, just to maintain their budgets. As this process was repeated year after year the ALF would get lower and nearer to the convergence figure. This led to the other function of the funding methodology, which was to bring about expansion of student numbers at lower unit costs.

Understanding incorporation as the 'marketisation' of education and training

Gleeson (1996) and many others argue that the incorporation of FE colleges was an attempt to create a national college sector through standardised funding, inspection and auditing within which colleges compete, in what is seen by government as an education and training market. This development in FE was reflected in other public services which were also experiencing 'new public management' (Leathwood 2000). While colleges had governors, the real line of accountability was to the FEFC. Therefore, within the context of marketisation competition there was a strong strand of national regulation (Gleeson 2001). Although centrally controlled, colleges existed in an education and training market. This led them to sometimes adopt a form of managerialism more associated with private companies in which students become customers (Elliott and Hall 1996).

The idea of a market is clear in economics; however, it is hard to see how FE colleges can operate in a market in any classic economic sense because the relationship between colleges and the vast majority of students is not determined by price (Harper 2000). As suggested elsewhere, college incorporation is perhaps better described as the creation of a 'quasi-market' within which incorporated colleges, schools, TECs and private sector trainers compete (Lucas and Mace 1999). A 'quasi-market' is where on the supply side there is competition between providers, but on the demand side purchasing power is not expressed in money terms but by a centralised regulatory agency influencing policy decisions (Le Grand and Bartlett 1993). Ultimately, the combined effect of the FEFC model of incorporation was the creation of 'bureaucratic markets', in which a centralised authority exercise control by making funding conditional on obeying rules and regulations that they have laid down (Lucas 1999).

Although the 'quasi-market' seems to be a grey area to economists, the belief in the efficiency of the marketisation of education and training was a fundamental ideological belief behind the Conservative government's project of incorporation. This included encouraging local bargaining on wages and conditions of service, and the planned introduction of vouchers for all post-16 learners in order to allow price to enter the picture for the first time (Unwin 1993). There were also proposals to create a common funding methodology for 16–19-year-olds in school sixth forms and FE colleges (DfEE 1996).[6]

Ainley (1993) argues that a 'quasi-market' is an increasing feature of the 'contract state' that applies to many public services. He contrasts this with the old 'corporate state', which met the needs of the social partners of the former mixed economy. The contract state represents a centralisation of power, which operates by franchise, contract and consumer charters untrammelled by social obligations, or even representative democracy.

The centralised and marketised system of funding had some unintended consequences (Leney *et al.* 1998). Ways of maximising units were learned very quickly by colleges, yet maximising funding by maximising units may benefit individual colleges but may not benefit the sector as a whole. The Hodge Report (Education and Employment Committee 1998) suggested that practices that simply maximise units of funding waste precious resources and that the FEFC should ensure that such 'perverse incentives' be dealt with through a process of simplifying the funding mechanism.

Following the election of a new Labour government in 1997, extra funds were given to the sector, with the announcement in 1998 of an 8.2 per cent cash increase for FE colleges, with efficiency gains being held (with HE) at 1 per cent per annum (Crequer 1998).[7] Consequently, with the arrival of the new government, the 'marketisation of FE' was replaced by a new combination of quasi-market involving the old FEFC methodology, alongside more state and regional planning with a new emphasis on co-operation between institutions. This new stage for FE colleges only lasted some three years as the government replaced the FEFC with a new Learning and Skills Council in April 2001 (DfEE 1999b).[8]

Assessing the FEFC model of incorporation

The problem of assessing the effects of the movement from a historically local and variable level of funding to a standardised national system lies in trying to disentangle the effects of incorporation, the historically different funding levels when colleges were under LEA control and the problem of meeting student needs which vary socially, geographically and financially (Chambers 1995). The FE college sector during the period of incorporation went through a rapid change, yet, as indicated earlier, incorporation was not a clean break with the past and had many points of continuity. The FEFC funding methodology may have represented some important advances on past practice but there is evidence that it had contradictory effects on different colleges (and departments).

Many of the colleges with higher ALFs were to be found in inner cities with student populations that required exceptional levels of support (Chambers 1995). They were also likely to have been colleges that had many different sites and were therefore expensive to run. These inner-city colleges claimed that the FEFC image of the incorporated college was located somewhere in 'middle England' and did not appear to take seriously the problems of colleges in deprived urban areas (Spours and

Lucas 1996). These differing experiences of incorporation – between high and low ALF, rural and urban colleges – create difficulties in analysing the benefits and disadvantages of incorporation.

Another problem in analysing incorporation lies in the changing views about the FEFC model of incorporation. Many principals in FE colleges were originally well disposed towards incorporation (FEFC 1993), although some subsequently looked back to the 'halcyon days' of LEA control (Lumby and Tomlinson 2000). In the climate of tension between colleges and LEAs following the 1998 Education Reform Act, many college managers thought that there could be benefits under incorporation as a national organisation that would not be available if colleges remained under local political control. This initially positive disposition towards the FEFC in the first year of incorporation, was reinforced when college budgets were relatively unaffected because the FEFC funding model was not yet operational. However, attitudes became more critical over the next few years as the resource implications of incorporation became increasingly evident. The hope that incorporation would simply be an extension of LMC introduced in the 1998 Education Act was soon lost as cuts in expenditure worked their way through college systems. Furthermore, staff perceptions were being shaped by a bitter and protracted dispute about contracts, the problems of meeting growth targets, the impact of cost reductions, and a wave of redundancies. This was particularly prevalent in those colleges with high ALFs. The 95 per cent of college principals supporting option 'E' during FEFC consultations (FEFC 1993) rapidly declined.[9] According to one principal the supporters who entered the 'Faustian bargain' with the FEFC and 'leaped smiling over the cliff' (Perry 1997: 3) soon became characterised by splits and divisions according to high and low ALF colleges, high franchise and low franchise colleges, big and small, urban and rural and commercially focused versus community focused FE colleges. In these circumstances FE colleges appear to have moved from their traditional fragmentation to a sector characterised by competition and division, as they competed for units of funding to improve 'efficiency' and lower the ALF.

Any analysis of incorporation should distinguish between two different dimensions. First, there is a distinction between incorporation as a particular form of public ownership and control, and the actual funding methodology, which has given incorporation its particular form; second, consideration needs to be given to the distinction between the funding mechanism itself and the overall level of funds allocated by the government to the FE sector. Cuts in public expenditure were already affecting colleges prior to incorporation (as well as other public services). Perhaps the 'efficiency gains' forced upon the sector are more important than the funding methodology itself.

The experience of the period since FEFC incorporation would support the view that the choice and implementation of funding methodologies has a profound impact on the values and culture of colleges (Lumby and Tomlinson 2000). In general, few supporters of incorporation realised that a move away from the benign control of LEAs would mean so much regulation and pressure as the new funding body attempted to create a national sector. Many of those most critical of the past and most supportive of incorporation came to see that alongside the considerable gains during incorporation the funding methodology has proved to be far more problematic for colleges than was foreseen at the time (Perry 1997). When judged by qualitative and curricular criteria, worries emerged about the impact of cuts in courses, hours and class size (Withers 1999), the increasing use of part-time teaching staff (Mackney 1998) and the difficulty in funding part-time education and training for adults who may only achieve part of the qualification and not complete the whole programme (Leney *et al*. 1998).

During the period of incorporation, change was dominated by the need to make 'efficiency savings' and to bring down the average level of funding by expanding student numbers. FE staff complained that the auditing demands of the FEFC were 'out of control', creating 'a whole new industry to support it' (Leney *et al*. 1998: 24) as colleges directed increasing amounts of resources towards meeting FEFC data requirements.[10] While many colleges tried to find a balance between educational and financial considerations, the logic of the funding methodology and low level of overall funding to the sector forced colleges to take steps that were not always in the best interest of the students (FEFC 1996). This included cuts in course hours, rising redundancies for full-time staff and the increased use of part-time, sometimes agency, staff to save money.

By about 1997, many FE colleges were in a financial crisis due to the 'efficiency savings' of the previous years (Batey 1999). Reports such as those of Kennedy (1997) and Fryer (1997) all indicated that changes were required. However, the recommendations of the Education and Employment Committee (1998) indicated that the changes need not be fundamental, since the crisis in FE colleges was primarily one of the overall amount of funds being inadequate rather than the funding methodology or incorporation itself. By 1997 no serious commentators were suggesting that colleges should return to LEA control. However, the funding methodology and the form that college incorporation had taken were being more openly questioned (Randle and Bradey 1997).

Although the period of incorporation from 1993 to 1997 was one of financial crisis for FE colleges, the period can also be seen as having some positive benefits (Graham 1997). The effects of growth on the diversity of learner needs, and the influences of community and adult education traditions (combined with the FEFC's pressure to make more 'efficiency savings'), caused colleges to seek new, more flexible ways of delivering learning programmes and to become more responsive and flexible organisations (Drodge and Cooper 1997).[11] From this point of view, the period of incorporation up to the General Election in 1997 represented a period of further diversity and innovation, albeit market-driven, and relatively unplanned.

Incorporation also led to improved entry, guidance and learning support procedures and mechanisms (Leney *et al.* 1998). Many FE colleges extended learning centres and computer learning facilities, began to accredit prior learning, and introduced a variety of new flexible learning techniques (alongside traditional ones). As a result of the 'efficiency drive' associated with incorporation, FE college teaching staff experienced significant changes in their role and the demands made upon them (Ainley and Bailey 1997). These included increased 'class contact' hours under new contracts, extra demands regarding curriculum development, tutoring and responding to the increases in information required by the FEFC funding regime (Leney *et al.* 1998),[12] and the trend for colleges to employ more part-time, less qualified staff, not as a means of meeting student need but as a way of saving money (Williams 1998). Furthermore, some part-time staff were employed not as teachers but as assessors or instructors, all of which was a way to reduce unit costs (Gleeson 2001).[13]

Did incorporation create a coherent national FE college sector?

In 1995 FE colleges were catering for far more 16–19-year-olds than schools; they also catered for older students, with 76 per cent of all FEFC-funded students being over 24 years of age (AfC 1996). While it is widely accepted that full-time 16–19-year-olds have common sets of needs regardless of whether they are at school or college, adult students are far more diverse in their needs, many of which differ from those of younger students. They may need flexible modes of study that are locally available at different times of the day or evening, accreditation of prior learning, and childcare support (Derrick 1997). In providing for adults in the mid-1990s, colleges had to become more customer-oriented and more locally responsive in order to meet their diverse needs (Reeves 1995). However, the pressure from the FEFC to create a national sector, and the imperative to respond to local needs if they were to meet the growth targets set by the FEFC, caused confusion concerning the boundaries of the role and responsibility of FE colleges in relation to school sixth forms, TECs, higher education and LEA adult provision (Lucas *et al.* 1999).

Despite the fact that FE college incorporation was supported by the majority of college principals (Atkinson 1995), few realised that the move away from LEA control would mean so much FEFC regulation (Perry 1997). A number of issues seemed to stand in the way of FE colleges becoming a coherent national sector. Colleges appeared to be meant to cater for all and sundry – 16–19-year-olds, both academic and pre-vocational, adult returners, those on vocational courses, links with employers, access students, HE students, those with special needs, the socially excluded, basic skills provision and those not involved anywhere else. As part of the growing emphasis on lifelong learning, it seemed that if you were not in a school sixth form, at work or at university then you should be involved with the local college (DfEE 1998). Within this vision of FE colleges there was great diversity and excellence (Kennedy 1997) but alongside the virtues there were also potential pitfalls. The virtue is increased commitment to access and achievement for all, but the possible pitfalls are that FE colleges lack a clear strategic role, either nationally or locally (Green and Lucas 1999).

As the 1998 Education and Employment Committee indicated, the institutions contained within the FE sector were still very varied. Institutions such as sixth-form, specialist art and design and agricultural colleges might range from less than 500 to as many as 6,000 students. By contrast, very large tertiary and FE colleges might contain anywhere from 4,000 to over 20,000 students. Some colleges were predominantly 16–19 academic institutions, some offered higher education courses, others offered predominantly vocational courses, or little beyond level two qualifications (GCSE level) for part-time and full-time adults. Each type of college contained within it different cultures and traditions (Robson 1998), different conditions of service (Scott 2001), with different priorities given to staff development and requirements regarding initial teacher training. All of this undermined the development of a common concept of professional practice.

Ultimately the changes brought about by the FEFC model of incorporation failed to create, in any real sense, a national post-16 sector. This was despite the introduction of national inspection and audit controls laid down by the Further and Higher Education Act (FEFC 1992a; Harper 2000). The Education and Employment Committee recognised the lack of leadership and strategic direction given to FE colleges, and called on the government not only to increase the overall funds given to the FE sector but also to explain its strategic priorities to the FEFC.

Between 1993 and 1999, FE colleges were treated and funded as a national sector, and given a national profile. However, this period also saw a further increase in the diversity of learners and curriculum programmes. As FE colleges increased their student numbers, they further reflected the heterogeneous nature of local and regional needs. In this respect FE colleges became 'all things to all people', with no clarity of mission or distinct function to set them apart from competing institutions. Furthermore, colleges received mixed messages from national agencies. For example, FE colleges received funding to enable them to increase co-operation at a local level. But at the same time they still had to work within a funding system that encouraged competition with other colleges, schools and HE institutions for students (Graham 1997). Similarly colleges were urged and funded to widen participation and reach the socially excluded, while their core funding and the basis upon which they were ranked in league tables required them to give priority to retention and whole-course results.

The haphazard development described in this and the last chapter has left FE in an ambiguous position. Even defining what FE colleges predominantly offer is difficult, as no two colleges are the same and most have different traditions within them. FE colleges are perhaps best understood not as institutions with a clear identity, but as a number of segments existing in a disparate relationship to each other. Within this context, FE college teachers reflect the segmented nature of the sector and lack a clear professional identity (Robson 1999). FE colleges have become caught half-way between catering for 16–19-year-olds and adult returners, and between full-time students and part-time students. Furthermore, they offer vocational and academic courses, provide programmes such as HNDs as well as those geared to adults needing basic skills, and cater for those wishing to gain access to higher education. In other words, FE colleges can be seen as both preparatory and lifelong learning institutions, as institutions contributing to national training targets, and as organisations responsive to local needs. It is this legacy of diversity and lack of a clear strategic mission that distinguishes the FE sector so clearly from schools and universities.

Conclusion

The combination of the *ad hoc* historical development of the sector, described in chapter 1, and the 'marketisation' of FE colleges between 1993 and 1999 had profound effects on FE colleges and the practices of teachers within them. During incorporation, FE colleges changed from their existing diversity to a sector dominated by competition, division and greater national regulation. Incorporation encouraged competition for students between FE colleges themselves and other providers. This led to innovation and change that further increased the number and diversity of learners and curriculum programmes. At the same time during the expansion under incorporation FE colleges became 'all things to all people': caught between catering for and competing for 16–19-year-olds and adult returners, full-time and part-time students; offering a wide variety of vocational, academic, access and basic skills courses with no clarity of mission. This left the 'modern' FE college in an ambiguous position of 'strategic drift' (Green and Lucas 1999a). Alongside the growing diversity and divisions within the FE college sector, the incorporation of colleges and the FEFC funding method also brought with it greater national regulation, national inspection and public accountability, in common with other areas of the public sector.

The period of incorporation addressed by this chapter went through a number of changes. One way of analysing the FEFC model of incorporation is to view it in terms of a series of stages (Spours and Lucas 1996). The first stage arose as a consequence of the 1988 Education Act, which gave colleges a measure of independence from LEAs with changed governance and devolved budgets (Gleeson 2001). The second stage from 1993, the first year of incorporation, can be characterised as one of independence without the FEFC funding mechanism. This was followed by a third stage from 1994 to the DLE[14] crisis in January 1997.[15] This third stage was the period of high growth targets, efficiency savings, redundancies, growing use of part-time staff and the dispute over FE lecturers' contracts (Hill 2000). This represented the period of the 'marketisation' of FE.

The fourth period was when the old funding regime of unlimited growth and competition began to crumble and, with the election of a new government in mid-1997, some of the worst aspects such as the growth rates and efficiency saving targets associated with the 'marketisation' of FE were eased a little (Harper 2000). This period marked the beginning of the end of the policies upon which incorporation had been founded: competition and the unplanned dash for growth (Lumby and Tomlinson 2000). The rhetoric of competition was replaced by one of co-operation and efforts were made to bring about partnership at a structural level (FEFC 1998) with an agenda around social inclusion, widening participation and lifelong learning.

By the year 2000 the fourth period of incorporation was drawing to a close. The end of the FEFC, which gave incorporation its particular form, was in sight. The new fifth stage had been brought about by the Labour government's proposal to restructure the post-16 system. This was signalled in the White Paper *Learning to Succeed* (DfEE 1999b), which heralded fundamental change in the funding and strategic direction of the FE sector, discussed in the next chapter.

Notes

1   This is discussed in more detail in chapter 4.
2   The report claimed that by doing this, colleges could save £50 million per year.
3   The number of units generated by a student on a specific course is determined by a tariff which is reviewed each year by the FEFC's independent tariff committee, comprising sector representatives and an independent chair.
4   Each student enrolled attracts a certain number of units for the college in respect of enrolment, on-course costs and student achievement. The precise number of units will depend upon the course, the student's progress and achievement.
5   For younger students and those on low incomes.
6   This is now being developed by the new Learning and Skills Councils.
7   Although the process of national convergence continued.
8   The latest developments and the setting up of the Learning and Skills Councils are discussed in the next chapter.

9   During the FEFC consultations (FEFC 1992) a number of funding options were presented. Each option was examined and criticised and option E was strongly recommended in the consultation document.

10 This is also confirmed by the work of Graham (1997) and Hodkinson (1998) who suggest that the data requirements are an indication of the regulatory nature of the FEFC.

11 Which were being absorbed by FE colleges.

12 Such as the individual student record which was introduced by the FEFC for auditing purposes and as a means of tracking student achievement and progression.

13 The rise in the proportion of part-time teachers and the implications for FE colleges is discussed further in chapter 5.

14 The demand-led element of the FEFC was designed to promote growth in student numbers by funding student expansion over agreed targets at a lower tariff.

15 This became known as the 'DLE crisis' and occurred in early 1997. The crisis was triggered when the DfEE asked the FEFC how they intended to keep within their expenditure limits, as there was a massive expansion of student numbers. This expansion was far in excess of the figures envisaged by the DfEE, which thought uncontrolled franchising was to blame. In response the FEFC decided that the uncapped DLE element would have to cease immediately as the Treasury refused to fund the expansion in student numbers. The FEFC advised colleges that not all DLE claims would be met and also stopped colleges from entering into any new franchising commitments based on DLE funding.

3 A new era of planning and realignment?

From the FEFC to the Learning and Skills Council

It is probably true to say that in the last ten years or so there has been more regulation and government policy concerned with further education then ever before. This reflects the growing importance of the further education sector generally in terms of its importance to the economy, as a means of social inclusion and as engine for raising participation in education and training. As the Secretary of State for Education and Skills recently put it: 'the learning and skills sector has never been more important to the Government's agenda than it is today. ... We must give further education and training its proper place as a vital mainstream part of the education system' (DfES 2002: 2).

The election of a Labour government in 1997 did not bring about any immediate change for the further education sector. Funding was not increased in the first year, since the new government was pledged to staying within the spending limits of the previous administration. However, there was some improvement in funding levels in the second year of office. The Labour government's first clear signal to the post-16 system came a couple of years after their election, in the White Paper *Learning to Succeed* (DfEE 1999b). This heralded fundamental change in the funding regime and strategic direction of the FE sector. It set out plans to create a more coherent post-16 sector, by abolishing the FEFC and TECs and creating a single funding body called the national Learning and Skills Council (LSC). The LSC funding remit included the FE sector, school sixth forms and LEA-run adult and community education. Funding is co-ordinated and administered through 47 Local Learning and Skills Councils (LLSCs).

In attempting to deal with the diversity of FE college provision *Learning to Succeed* included proposals for separate inspection regimes for 16–19-year-olds and adults, as well as separate committees for 16–19-

year-olds and adults within the new Learning and Skills Council. Furthermore, it proposed, among other things, to simplify the system of funding to make it more responsive to the needs of learners and employers by funding four key elements: the recruitment of learners; retention; achievement; and combating social disadvantage. The government pledged to make the funding flexible enough to ensure that it could facilitate moving unemployed people into work, as well as funding curriculum changes such as 'Curriculum 2000' for the 16–19 age group (DfEE 2000).

The Learning and Skills Council replaced the FEFC on 1 April 2001 and took over responsibility for all post-16 education and training, including work-based training in England (excluding higher education). This new LSC sphere of activity was renamed the 'learning and skills sector'. The LSC pledged to introduce a new funding system for FE and sixth-form colleges by 2002/3 and promised to operate a safety net for the transitionary period. Both of these pledges were carried out. The FEFC inspectorate was replaced by OFSTED, which had its responsibility for schools inspection extended to include 16–19-year olds in colleges. A new Adult Learning Inspectorate (ALI) was established to inspect adult learning. This included inspection of work-based provision (replacing the Training Standards Council). Lastly, the old careers, youth and probation services were replaced by an umbrella organisation known as Connexions.

It is still unclear how strategic and integrated the LSC approach will eventually be. At the time of writing, the new Chief Executive of the LSC has pledged to reform the 47 LLSCs into nine regions covering the same areas as the government's regional development agencies, and to cut red tape and jargon (Nash 2003). The roles of the University for Industry, and the emerging Sector Skills Councils are as yet not clearly articulated in the new structure. Furthermore, there is little clarity concerning how higher education is to relate to the regional bodies.

The new funding arrangements

The old FEFC funding regime, while making some improvements, had many weaknesses. Some of these are identified in *Success for All* (DfES

Table 3.1 *Changes in responsibility from the FEFC to the LSC*

FEFC responsible for	LSC responsible for
• further education colleges	• further education colleges
• sixth-form and tertiary colleges	• sixth-form and tertiary colleges
• specialist colleges of agriculture and art and design	• specialist colleges of agriculture and art and design
• external institutions sponsored by FE colleges	• external institutions sponsored by FE colleges
• higher education delivering further education	• higher education delivering further education
• specialist designated institutions	• specialist designated institutions
	• work-based learning
	• government-supported training
	• LEA-funded adult and community education (non schedule 2)
	• school sixth forms
	Remit extended to
	• providing information, advice and guidance to adults
	• advising government on National Learning Targets
	• workforce development
	• education and business links

2002). This states that incorporation in 1993 did not establish a clear framework for accountability or standards and introduced a harsh national funding regime. Under this regime, colleges were forced to expand in order to cut costs, while other FE providers were subject to separate funding arrangements and little investment. A number of the problems that developed under the FEFC are still apparent today including:

- a culture of decision making within colleges and other providers which has been reactive to funding opportunities rather than based on a clear analysis of the organisations' distinctive mission and strengths;

- a wide variety of quality with an insufficient emphasis on standards, success rates and the development of excellence and too

much time spent by managers chasing and accounting for funding and not enough on raising standards and relevance of teaching and learning;

- patterns of provision are based on a history of competition and
  opportunistic provider expansion. There has been little strategic
  planning for the coherent longer term development of the supply
  side to provided type and quality of provision local learners and
  employers want;

- within the sector, there is a workforce whose skill and career
  development has often been neglected. There has been unhealthy
  levels of casualisation and insufficient emphasis on improving
  professional skills, on updating subject or occupational knowledge and on developing skills for the future;

- a legacy of under investment in the capital infrastructure with too
  much learning taking place in unattractive and inefficient buildings and lack of investment in updating of vocational training
  facilities.

(DfES 2002: 5)

In answer to these rather damming criticisms of the FEFC funding
method the Learning and Skills Act 2000 brought about two fundamental
changes. First it allowed the LSC to fund a much wider set of institutions,
encouraging more strategic planning and co-operation between providers
in the learning and skills sector.[1] The new LSC's remit covers funding FE
and sixth-form colleges, school sixth forms, government-supported training, workplace learning (where it meets LSC standards) and funding
adult and community education with LEAs.

Second, the LSC changed the funding methodology itself. Most
markedly this was done by scrapping units of resource and replacing
them with cash payments based on full-time equivalents.[2] In short, the
LSC abandoned the use of units for different stages of a student's learning and replaced them with national rates reflecting inflation for courses.

Table 3.2 *Changes in funding from the FEFC to LSC*

FEFC	LSC
Entry units	No entry payment
On programme units	Base rate paid in £s for courses
Achievement units (7% under FEFC)	10% achievement deducted if student fails, 20% for work-based learning
Units of funding	Base rate for courses paid in £s
Cost weighting factor for courses (Tariff)	Programmes weighting, i.e. 30% for C courses, 60% for D courses, etc.
London Weighting factor	Area costs
Additional support	Additional learning support
One-year funding cycle	Three-year funding cycle

These are not calculated in units but are set in pounds. The new funding method also has different programmes weighted by the National Rates Advisory Group (NRAG) that takes account of the programme costs, the relative disadvantage of students, and area costs.

Table 3.3 *Transition to the new funding formula*

Provision	2000/1	2001/2	2002/3	2003/4	2004/5
School sixth forms	LEAs	LEA fair funding formula	new funding formula	common funding formula	common funding formulas
FE colleges	FEFC	FEFC formula retained	new funding formula	common funding formula	common funding formulas
Work-based learning	TECs	national formula introduced	funding approach reviewed		common funding formulas
Adult and community learning	LEAs	LEA adult learning plans funded	LEA adult learning plans funded		common funding formulas

Source: Gravatt 2001

The transition to this new formula was planned to be introduced within four years, with the LSC promising that school sixth forms were guaranteed to receive at least the same funding total of the past year in the first two years of the new funding method. There was also provision of a safety net for colleges whose funding was reduced solely because of the new formula in the first year. The plan is that by 2004/5 all providers will have a common funding formula.

Another feature of the new funding regime was that the national LSC proposed to allocate growth targets (with a claw-back if targets are not achieved).[3] Local LSCs were also to receive funds to allocate to individual providers according to their strategic area plans.

Since *Success for All* there have been many circulars and changes. A very important one, issued in October 2003, was *Plan Led Funding for Further Education* (LSC 2003a). This consultation document stresses the importance of a 'trust relationship' within the context of the planning framework established by *Success for All*. Such a relationship is to be based on a more selective and targeted approach, consistent with the government's wider principles of 'intervention in inverse proportion to success'. In other words, a 'light touch' was proposed for those doing well and more intervention for those colleges that were doing badly. The document consulted on key changes such as a more transparent relationship between funding, planning, recruitment, retention and achievement. It proposed to end retrospective claw-back and replace traditional audits with a simpler 'regularity audit', which included the abolition of intermediate census dates and a new approach to fees to enable regional planning and level-two entitlements.[4] In short it was proposed that funding should be 'plan-led' with bonuses for good provision and sanctions for the poor ones.

Another feature of these arrangements is worth noting. As outlined above, FE colleges were now part of what government agencies called the 'learning and skills sector'. There are real dangers that FE colleges will once again get lost within other priorities and policies of the new learning and skills sector and continue their 'strategic drift' (Green and Lucas 1999). Such a view has been endorsed by the Chief Inspector of

Adult Learning Inspectorate (ALI), who noted how OFSTED/ALI college inspection reports went almost unnoticed by policy makers and the press.

> It was I suppose inevitable that change from being the 'FE sector' to one part of 'the learning and skills sector' would have caused a lowering of the profile of colleges. I for one was unprepared for its extent and speed
>
> (Sherlock 2003: 1)

Such comments reflect a view that the FE college sector was losing the higher profile it achieved under the FEFC as it becomes part of a much larger and more diverse learning and skills sector (discussed in chapter 7).

Importantly, this new learning and skills sector is heavily influenced by employer-led bodies. Both the national and local LSC are employer-led, as are the emerging Sector Skills Councils that are to replace national training organisations.[5] The government claims that by putting employers in the 'driving seat' the sector will become consumer-driven which, in turn, will lead to finding new solutions for the learning needs of businesses. What the government used to call 'employer-led bodies' are now described as 'led by leading employers' (Hook 2003). What this shift in emphasis represents is hard to say, although it does seem to imply that the reason for the poor record of employer-led bodies is that they failed to attract leading employers of the highest quality and that this is a key to their success (Bewick 2003). What is clear is that the government was determined that employers should articulate their skills need and 'drive what education and training is provided by colleges, universities and schools' (Campbell 2003: 18). However, while the government reflects the same faith in the business community as past governments, what is expected of employers is not to set up markets and competition but to plan provision on a regional basis.

As I noted in chapter 2, Ainley (1993) characterises the policy of the Conservative governments of the 1980 and 1990s as instigating the 'contract state'. The 'contract state' sought to create markets and competition as an alternative to the post-war centralist 'corporate state'. Subsequent governments seemed to be looking for a 'third way' between the models of 'corporate' and 'contract state'. As far as education and training is concerned it would seem that they neither wish to take direct responsibility for the strategic planning of post-16 education as in the 'corporate state', nor leave it to the market and competition. Instead, national and regional unelected employer-led bodies mediate between government and the providers. Unlike in the past, these bodies are given responsibility for the strategic planning of post-16 education and training with the state acting as a sort of 'benign umpire'.

In this scenario, the government establishes regulations, armies of quality assurance and inspection regimes and employer-led quangos. However, central government does not take direct responsibility or get involved in detailed planning or regulation. Perhaps the phrases 'umpire state' or 'regulatory state' are more appropriate descriptions when it comes to analysing early twenty-first century government policy on post-compulsory education and training. It could also be argued that giving employers responsibility to set up markets and enhance competition makes some sense, but to give employers responsibility for strategic planning of many private and public organisations would not seem to be playing to their strengths.

The implications of *Success for All*

In a speech launching the discussion document, *Success for All*, the Secretary of State for Education suggested that the FE sector needed to change its image and improve performance because it was vital to the economy and to government targets for the expansion of higher education (Clark 2002). He stated that although there had been significant advances in some areas, college inspections had shown that 59 per cent were judged to be inadequate or required partial re-inspection. The obvious message was that the core purpose of *Success for All* was that of raising standards across the sector.

The strategy focused around four main elements of reform. The first was 'meeting needs and improving choice'. This focused on meeting local needs and how to work with other providers in each area. Under this

Table 3.4 *Objectives and themes of Success for All*

Objectives	Themes
• provide education and training through the new 14–19 age phase • increase progression into higher education • help people improve their basic skills • widen participation for adults • help employers invest in the skills of their staff	• widen choice in local area • improve responsiveness through area reviews • prioritise teaching and learning • further the professional development of teachers, leaders, trainers and support staff • develop a framework for quality and success

Source: LSC 2003

element strategic area reviews led by the local LSCs will ensure that the right mix and quality of provision is in place to meet learner, employer and community needs. This requires providers in each area to be clear about their contribution and play to their particular strengths. The document suggested that there is clearly more than one form of area organisation and co-operation. For example, the general FE college may be the right model in rural areas. However, different types of provision should be looked at in each area and, in particular, distinct 16–19 provision in the form of sixth-form colleges or centres is often mentioned. In short, it required all providers to review their educational and training mission in relation to area needs, demonstrating their excellence and strengths.

The second element of reform was, 'putting teaching training and learning at the heart of what we do'. This heading focused on raising standards and sharing good practice. Within this element, the work of the new Standards Unit was central. *Success for All* states that the Standards Unit will work with practitioners and partners, identify and disseminate effective practice, develop new teaching and learning frameworks to support teachers, improve the provision of training for teachers and develop a coherent national e-learning strategy. This is discussed further in chapter 7.

Third, *Success for All* aimed at 'developing leader teachers, lecturers and support staff for the future'. It proposed that the number of qualified teachers should increase and that there should be greater access to continuing professional development, which should become part of colleges' three-year plans, agreed with the LSC (this is also discussed more fully in chapter 7). Under this heading, it was also proposed to develop an employer-led Sector Skills Council for the learning and skills sector to assess workforce development, to establish a new leadership college for the sector and to introduce rewards linked to performance for FE college teachers.

The fourth element was 'developing a framework for quality and success'. This new framework for success was accompanied by considerable increases in funding for the sector, three-year funding agreements and a new system of targets and performance management. The objective of the introduction of performance management was to invest in action to 'raise standards, identify and reward excellence, identify poor practice and reduce bureaucracy' (DfES 2002b: 41). This new system of performance management (which did not include school sixth forms) set 'floor targets' for learner success that take into account the learning context. Providers who fell below the minimum performance level needed to put forward plans for improvement and target dates for improvements to be met. Those who did better than the floor targets will get extra funding and may secure 'learning and skills beacon status', the benefit of which will be less frequent and less intense inspection and a requirement to share their good practice with others.

As mentioned above, the launching of *Success for All* was accompanied by increased government funding for FE colleges, albeit with many strings attached. As the Learning and Skills Council stated:

> Funding for FE will increase by 19% in real terms by 2005/6. While the consolidation of separate funding streams, plus new funding will mean that FE providers will receive 10% increase in funding rates in 2003/4. ... All subsequent increases will be linked to performance. Colleges and providers of excellence will receive more then those who just deliver plans and achieve targets and those performing poorly will receive still less but will benefit from intervention and support to help them to improve, or other appropriate action.
>
> (LSC 2003: paragraph 15/16)

Alongside the increase in the quantum given to FE the implication of the three-year plans in relation to area reviews take on great importance as they included financial forecasts, self-assessment documents, post-inspection reports, human resource plans and other key areas. Also included in the plans are how to increase customer focus and build closed relationships with employers, as well as improving teaching and learning linked to clear targets. Colleges with agreed three-year plans get 2 per cent extra funding in return from the LSC; colleges which fail to agree a plan with their local LSC will not get it. Such is the nature of the new regime.

Together with the increased funding there was to be a greater emphasis on improving the quality of teaching and learning. The emphasis on improving the quality of teaching and management reflected concerns raised in inspection reports that the standard of teaching in sixth-form and tertiary colleges was higher than in general FE colleges. In 2003 the Chief Inspector of ALI reported that alongside much good practice in learner support and committed teachers, of the 73 general FE colleges inspected, one in five was judged to be inadequate, management was weak and college connections with employers was frail (Sherlock 2003). Furthermore, only 33 per cent of construction and 37 per cent of information technology was considered good or outstanding and, as OFSTED observed (Singleton 2003), weaker colleges were not able to improve on inspection findings, improve teaching or ensure that students get on the right courses.[6]

According to the then Chief Executive of the Learning and Skills Council[7]

> Attention needs to be given to improving teaching and training, to the effectiveness of learning and of engaging the education sector with local and regional businesses and employers. We intend to tackle these issues. Our proposed framework of action aims to recognise and reward success, promote improvement and provide support where it is needed.
>
> (LSC 2003: foreword)

Within this broad aim it seems clear that for colleges the Strategic Area Reviews (SARs) were to be given great importance because they were fundamental in bringing about real changes in the patterns of delivery. Indeed, as the Chief Executive of the LSDA suggested (Hughs 2002), FE colleges were to think much more strategically, focusing on breadth and specialisation and on how to shift from being a local provider in competition with others to being a local strategic player. Hughs argues that vague mission statements will no longer be adequate, since under the new regime colleges must make specific statements concerning their strategic role within the area, focusing on their particular curriculum strengths and whether to provide 16–19 education as well as catering for the older age group.

The challenges involved in strategic area reviews were illustrated in a report published by the LSDA (Edam *et al.* 2003), which aimed at giving guidance to the DfES on the conduct of SARs. The report suggested that current policy changes in documents such as *Success for All* and the change to a single mechanism for all publicly funded post-16 provision created strong imperatives away from the competition of the past towards collaboration between providers. These collaborative imperatives required planned provision across an area and cohesion across the phases of school, further and higher education. The report presented a theoretical model to illuminate ways of creating a post-16 typology map. At an institutional level, current education and training arrangements were analysed on a simple, broad-based–specialised axis with very large all-age institutions on one extreme and specialist colleges on the other. Sixth-form colleges and work-based learning fell somewhere in between. (This is represented on the horizontal axis in figure 3.1.) When looking at provision in collaborative terms the authors conceived of illustrating local forms of arrangement and co-operation in terms of a tight–loose axis. This axis expresses the degree of formality of any collaborative arrangements, with small-scale arrangements between a school and a college on one extreme and very formal large-scale arrangements leading to mergers between providers on the other. Co-marketing and joint ventures fell somewhere in the middle. (This is illustrated on the vertical axis in figure 3.1.)

Such a way of classifying organisational arrangements may be helpful in accessing the tasks of strategic area reviews. However, as the authors readily admit, such a simplification did not take into account the full complexity of the provision within an existing area. For example,

Figure 3.1 *Planning area collaboration: a post-16 typology map*

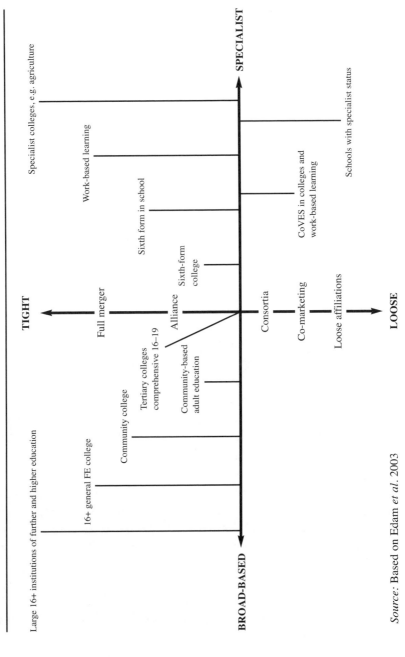

Source: Based on Edam *et al.* 2003

specialisation and broad-based provision can take different forms, such as being curriculum-based (predominantly vocational or academic or level of study) or learner group-based (16–19-year-olds or adults). In other words, a sixth-form college specialising in 16–19-year-olds can, on the one hand, be broad-based in terms of curriculum programmes, offering entry level qualifications alongside vocational and academic courses, yet on the other hand it can be seen as specialist because it caters for a specific age group. Equally, predominantly specialist adult institutions may be all part-time, with little above level 2 qualifications (GCSE level) or they may be institutions offering a wide range up to entry courses for higher education. In other words, adult institutions can specialise in providing access to higher education for full-time students or adult basic skills programmes for part-time adults. Such complexities will vary between and within areas according to their history. This makes strategic planning between existing providers in an area quite difficult even where you have the goodwill of institutions and the community.

While the vertical axis is also helpful, the collaboration between providers will vary from area to area. As a report on improving collaboration in one London borough pointed out (Bromley *et al.* 1999), competition between providers in an area has existed for a long time,[8] resulting in a culture of competition and a lack of trust and respect between key provider players at 16+. There are many factors militating against collaboration and these are reflected in targets of educational achievement expressed in league tables and the like, and in the culture created since 1993 that positively encourages competition through the 'marketisation' of education and training (Lucas 1999). It is unlikely that a successful sixth-form college and strong sixth-form provision in schools would find it easy to collaborate, or that schools with weak sixth-form provision would agree to go 11–16. Such changes arouse strong feelings. There are all sorts of legal and political factors involved in bringing about such collaboration and planning. Much will depend on the existing provision, ranging from 16–19 arrangements, adult and community education, the policies of the former training and enterprise councils to the political leadership given by LEAs. Furthermore, City Technology Colleges will need to be considered alongside a host of work-based learning providers that have little if any history of collaboration with other educational institutions.

Neither is regional planning straightforward. As an LSC consultation document illustrated, there are many local, regional and sectoral stake-holders to plan with. These include 'RDAs, Skills for Business Network, Small Business Services (SBS) and Job Centre plus'; furthermore, 'local LSCs will also be members of the new Regional Skills Partnerships, bro-kered by RDAs which will build on the existing Frameworks for Regional Employment Action Zones (FRESAs) (LSC 2003a: paragaph 52).'

How such a complex layer of bodies is going to plan together is 'chal-lenging'. In the absence of clear strategic political leadership by central and local government are the hard-pressed national and local employer-led LSCs really up to the task? Furthermore, how long will all these agen-cies continue? As Evans (2002) points out, organisations for education and training are littered with bodies that have been changed and abol-ished by a plethora of government departments and other players.[9]

Conclusion

The challenges faced by Strategic Area Reviews are not an argument against greater collaboration: on the contrary. It is simply that a big gap exists between the good intensions from the DfES and others and the detailed plans of how to proceed. How the new Learning and Skills Council and the Standards Unit will work in practice remains to be seen. They both have incredibly wide and varied responsibilities in the context of a fragmented planning structure, the continuing 'voluntarist' role of employers in the whole exercise (Hyland and Merrill 2003) and the lack of detailed political responsibility taken by central government.

A major issue concerns the ability of the employer-led national and 47 local learning and skills councils to bring about collaboration and area planning. LSCs and their lead employers have little experience in bring-ing about collaboration between government bodies, schools, colleges, work-based providers and universities. The areas that LLSCs cover are not always rationally focused on some form of identifiable area provision;

some simply reflect former TEC interests. Furthermore, many general and specialised providers draw students from across LLSC areas, and universities are in any case not under the auspices of the LSC. While funding can be a strong lever to bring about more planning and collaboration, it cannot be a substitute for getting broad agreement between the providers, LEAs and others. Getting such agreement is not context- or value-free (Edam *et al.* 2003) and will take time and firm strategic political commitment to achieve.

Notes

1 For a detailed explanation and critique of the FEFC funding methodology see Lucas 1999; Leney *et al.* 1998; Lucas *et al.* 1999.

2 A legal distinction remains between the institutions it funds by grants (schools and colleges) and private training providers that it funds by contract.

3 In the LSC consultations it proposed that retrospective clawbacks are ended (LSC 2003a).

4 Level two entitlements refer to the Government policy that all fees are paid for adults who are trying to reach a level two (GCSE or equivalent) qualification or below.

5 At the time of writing only a few Sector Skills Councils have been agreed. It has been estimated that between 20 and 30 SSCs are to be set up to replace the 72 National Training Organisations. There is a proposal for a Lifelong Learning Sector Skills Council which will include the FE college sector (see chapter 7).

6 The ALI inspectorate also found nearly half the grades awarded to work-based learning were less than satisfactory.

7 Who was replaced by Mark Haysom in September 2003.

8 This competition and lack of trust pre-dates incorporation in 1993 and the Thatcher era.

9 Evans *et al.* (2002) ask if this ceaseless changing landscape in education and training might not be viewed as a form of displacement activity.

Part 2

THE TRAINING AND PROFESSIONAL DEVELOPMENT OF TEACHERS IN FURTHER EDUCATION

4 FE teacher education: a history of neglect

Introduction

The second part of this book examines the historical development of teacher education and professional development of further education teachers.[1] This chapter looks at three main periods: first, teaching and teacher training from the late nineteenth century to 1944; second, the period from 1944 to 1990; and third, the position of initial teacher education and staff development just prior to the incorporation of FE colleges in 1993. Chapters 5 and 6 look at two further periods, 1993 to 1999 and the present policy context.

This chapter highlights the haphazard and uneven approach there has been to the professional development of teachers in FE. This is not just a result of successive governments' 'benign neglect' (Young *et al.* 1995). It has also been reinforced by the attitudes of many teachers and managers in colleges themselves, who believed that vocational/technical or subject expertise was in itself an adequate basis for teaching (Tipton 1973). The inheritance of these assumptions, combined with the absence of any obligation to gain teaching qualifications, led to the tendency of technical and FE college teachers to identify primarily with their vocational, industrial and, later, their subject expertise. This contributed to the isolation of FE teachers within their specialisms, thus reinforcing the diverse and fragmented teaching and learning traditions which still characterise FE today (Gleeson and Shain 1999).[2]

Teaching and teacher education from the late nineteenth century to 1944

Records concerning the quality of teaching, and discussions about teacher training for vocational, technical and further education during the nineteenth century are scant and unclear (McNair Report 1944). There are some records of debates within governmental bodies about the teaching of technical subjects in schools, but by and large vocational education was not considered or given any real priority by central government in the nineteenth century (Bratchel 1968; Barnett 1986).

In the nineteenth century, the dominant view was that a very basic education was considered enough for aspiring apprentices, and that the best learning environment for a craft apprenticeship was the workplace (Aldrich 1999). Apprenticeships remained the major training route in the late nineteenth and early to mid-twentieth century. In the apprenticeship tradition, the major responsibility for training, which consisted of observation and mimicking, fell to skilled men, with employers not usually playing a major role or even choosing all the apprentices (Summerfield and Evans 1990). For industry, the system was a cheap way of training labour and imparting skills. Few trades saw any need for technical understanding and knowledge, considering it irrelevant for the ordinary worker, although useful for good foremen (Clark 1999). The Royal Commission on Technical Instruction of 1882–4 reinforced this view, stating that the 'system of instruction for the great body of our foremen and workmen' was in the main 'not desirable to disturb' (quoted in Cotgrove 1958: 34). The report seems to confirm that most 'practical men' and employers were of one opinion – that theory or generalisable knowledge was not necessary, or to be trusted (Argles 1964).

As the London County Council (LCC) confirmed in 1892, obstacles to technical training lay among management and employees alike: 'in the numerous small chemical and colour works in East London and the tanneries of Bermondsey there is a rooted disbelief, shared between management and men alike, in the value of such training' (Argles 1964: 37). This led to a reluctance on the part of employers to give day-release to their employees (Edwards 1961). The number of day-release students did increase between the wars but they remained small in absolute numbers, with training for employees 'suffering the same disease it had in the nineteenth century – unimaginative management' (Argles 1964: 70).

Where formal technical and vocational education did take place, it attracted some criticism as to its quality. There are records of complaints about the quality of science teaching in a report by the Select Committee on Scientific Instruction 1867–8 (Cotgrove 1958). The committee stated that because of the low professional status of technical education there was a dire shortage of science teachers, and the provision of teachers for 'trade classes' was even worse, with much of the teaching being 'slip-shod, unmethodical and unsystematic' (Argles 1964). Furthermore, there seemed to be some confusion between the role of workshop instructors and teachers: 'workshop instructors really belong to the teaching staff and provide a great range of practical instructions[3] ... yet receive no training or even support from college managers and were mostly left to their own devices' (Richardson 1939: 127).

In 1902/3, the London County Council Technical Education Board also pointed to the extreme difficulty of obtaining teachers who had practical knowledge, who understood scientific principles and who possessed the ability to teach (LCC 1903). When it came to education after the school leaving age, which was still 12, little was said, except instruction should be of 'a more practical nature'.

Sadler, in a report on evening technical schools in Liverpool published in 1904, found the effectiveness of the schools very poor for a number of reasons. First, the instruction was extremely elementary and was largely devoted to making up for work that should have been done at school. Second, that indifference and carelessness on the part of students and teachers, sometimes coupled with awkward working hours, meant average attendance of only 50 per cent. Third, 'rigid external examination syllabuses made the teaching unimaginative and constrained' (Sadler, in Argles 1964: 63). Furthermore, those students who did attend evening classes often dropped out either because their levels of literacy were so low that they could not cope with the content of the classes or because they found the drudgery of learning the basics unbearable (Edwards 1961).

The shortage of good teachers was frequently blamed for low student attainment and student retention, as well as the 'difficulty of teaching classes composed of people of all ages and varying attainments' (Edwards 1961: 19). At the turn of the twentieth century there was no institution or qualification for training technical teachers (Evans 1975). The method adopted to obtain teachers was to recruit from the best students who had taken the courses (Edwards 1961).

The 1918 Fisher Act, which required all Local Education Authorities to provide free and obligatory day continuation schooling for those leaving school at 14 (discussed in chapter 1), could have brought about a more systematic approach to the training of teachers. However, the compulsory element of the Act was lost due to a lack of strategic leadership by central government (Green 1990) within the context of the economic depression of the 1920s (Bristow 1970). During this period, there was also some development of adult non-vocational education. However, the school sector was seen as a much higher priority than technical colleges, and all areas of education were squeezed through the expenditure cuts in the inter-war era (Foden 1992). On the whole, post-school education reverted to its pre-war pattern and remained predominately a system of evening classes (Bratchel 1968). Only fragmentary historical records exist of these evening classes (Edwards 1961), with almost none concerning the quality and training of teachers.

Until 1944, teacher training for vocational and technical education did not really exist in any form that would be recognisable today. Most teachers in further education prior to 1944 were part-time, with a very small core of full-time staff. Concern about the extensive use of part-time staff was commented upon: 'The proportion of full-time to part-time staff is a matter of some importance. The part-time teacher requires supervision ... It would appear that there is a certain ideal proportion that should not be exceeded' (Richardson 1939: 152).

Between the two world wars, some sandwich full-time and part-time courses were provided for technical teachers by LEAs and were accredited by awarding bodies such as City and Guilds (Foden 1992). Regional Advisory Councils and some Boards of Education also provided some short courses for teachers in adult education (Elsdon 1975). In 1938 there were 4,000 full-time technical teachers (Robson 1998) from the 170 trades and occupations (McNair Report 1944) represented in technical colleges. Staff in the colleges tended to reflect the values and cultures of their trade and occupation (Venables 1967; Gleeson and Mardle 1980). Within these vocational institutions were many diverse practices and cultures, sometimes a hostility to other trades and occupations (Carlton *et al.* 1971), and a resistance to addressing issues of teaching and learning. This legacy was to influence attitudes and the culture of many technical and FE college teachers for the rest of the century

The nineteenth- and the early twentieth-century inheritance was that teaching in technical colleges was more associated with 'training' or 'instruction', the transmission of skills, and with 'mastering' a craft through practice (Richardson 1939). On the whole, most vocational education took place through apprenticeship, which assumed that a craft or trade was best learnt 'on the job' by copying 'good' practice from a skilled and experienced practitioner. These assumptions were reproduced in technical colleges that were 'thrust as it were, into a corner of our national system and treated as, at best, mere useful adjuncts of the workshop or the mine' (Perry 1930: 57).

The growth of teaching qualifications in further education, 1944 to 1990

Chapter 1 described the considerable growth of day-release employees entering technical colleges in the war years. Coinciding with the growth of technical college students, an official government committee chaired by Sir Arnold McNair expressed the view in 1944 that subject expertise and vocational experience were important but were not in themselves a qualification for teaching, that the technical or vocational teacher needed teacher training, and furthermore: 'Technical Education in this country has never received the attention it deserves, and there has hitherto been no systematic provision for recruitment or training of technical teachers (McNair Report 1944: para. 381).

The McNair Report criticised the general quality of teaching as 'dull', with no effort being made to use new methods. The qualities needed for teaching in technical colleges were identified by the committee as: a sound general education; a high standard of subject, skill or craft knowledge; and the ability to teach as opposed to simply being an instructor of passive pupils (Bratchell 1968). The report went on to deny any conflict between technical, vocational or liberal education and stated that the technical college teacher was as worthy of recognition as teachers in any other sector. This was the first official government report to recognise this.

The report recorded that in 1938 there were 4,000 full-time technical teachers, although the number of teachers employed in technical colleges during the war years is not known. Hall (1994) estimates that the number of day-release students rose from 42,000 in 1939 to 150,000 by the end of the war, representing a growth in excess of 300 per cent. The McNair Report speculated that to meet the growing demand for further education 500 new full-time teachers would be needed each year. The report recommended that in order to achieve this, a planned approach was needed to replace the 'haphazard and opportunist' approach of the past 'with nothing systematic being done to provide for the needs of the future' (McNair 1944: para. 400). McNair recommended that FE teacher training should be mainly in-service in character, but that one-year pre-service courses should also be developed.

In many respects McNair laid the basis of today's FE college initial teacher education (ITE) system, proposing that initial teacher education should be in four units: the principles of education; the principles of teaching; the study of students' interests, outlook, environment, etc.; and industrial and commercial contexts. Teaching would also be observed by skilled practitioners. However, the training of teachers was to remain voluntary, although salary increments were to be introduced to encourage participation. With the impetus of the McNair Report and the 1944 Education Act, which charged local authorities to provide further education in their areas (Bratchell 1968), the first colleges specialising in vocational education were opened in London in 1946, in Bolton in 1947, and in Huddersfield in 1947 (Hall 1990).

In 1956, the government published a White Paper entitled *Technical Education* (MoE 1956). This highlighted the importance of expanding technical and vocational education and the supply of teachers for further education, noting that since 1945 there had been an impressive expansion in further education, with 500 colleges established throughout the country (Bratchell 1968). Following closely on the White Paper, a report known as the 'Willis Jackson Report' (MoE 1957), entitled *The Supply and Training of Teachers in Technical Colleges*, revealed that there had been a large increase in the teaching force in technical colleges. There were an estimated 11,000 full-time teachers and some 40,000 part-time teachers. Only 300 places were available in three FE teacher training colleges at the time, with universities exclusively concerned with training teachers for primary and secondary schools (MoE 1957). The Willis Jackson Report concluded that two-thirds of the teaching load was carried by full-time staff employed in technical colleges. Of the full-time teaching staff, only about one-third had received teacher training. Of the one-third of full-time staff who were teacher-trained, most taught subjects which were traditionally taught in schools, such as maths, science and general subjects. Very few teachers recruited from industry or those involved in vocational education had any teacher training. Importantly, if part-time staff were included, much less than one-fifth of the courses in technical colleges in 1956 were taught by teachers who had any teaching qualification.

The Willis Jackson Report was followed up by a special standing committee dealing with initial teacher education for those working in technical colleges (MoE 1957). The committee sought to redress the imbalance of part-time to full-time teaching staff by recommending that by 1960/1 colleges would need an extra 7,000 full-time and 8,000 part-time teachers. The report, known as the 'Crowther Report' (MoE 1959), estimated that 75 per cent of the annual intake of full-time teachers were without training and proposed the expansion of full-time and part-time courses for technical college teachers and the establishment of a fourth college in Wolverhampton. This opened in 1961 (Peters 1977). The Report also indicated that success rates for part-time courses were as low as 6 per cent and rarely exceeded 50 per cent. It suggested that a tutorial system for students be put in place and further recommended the establishment of a residential staff college and the appointment of a permanent advisory committee on the supply and training of technical college teachers.

Ten years after the Willis Jackson Report and eight years after

Crowther, *The Supply of Trained Teachers in Further Education* (known as the 'Russell Report') was published (1966). It identified some improvements, but reported that still less than one-third of the FE and technical college teaching force was teacher-trained. When faced with making recommendations to increase the proportion of trained teachers in FE colleges, it recognised that there was no qualified teaching status, as in schools, and took the position that this was not achievable in FE and technical colleges. The standing committee recommended that all new entrants teaching 15–18-year-olds should be teacher-trained within three years of their appointment. This was to be implemented by local education authorities by 1969. This recommendation, however, was promptly rejected by the Secretary of State, who instead recommended a continuation of the voluntary system, although with more incentives to achieve teaching qualifications, in the form of salary increments and secondments (Bratchell 1968).

Even though the government stopped short of taking statutory measures concerning teacher education for FE college teachers, the expansion of students at colleges and the growing numbers of staff teaching the 'new FE curriculum' (establishing new teaching and learning traditions) did lead to some improvement in the proportion of those gaining teacher education (Bristow 1970). How good or bad the teaching in FE colleges was in the 1960s and 1970s is hard to tell, as very little research has been carried out (Cantor *et al.* 1995). It is known that further education colleges still had the old legacy of the vocational teacher with industrial and trade expertise being seen as a sufficient qualification to teach (Gleeson and Mardle 1980). Newer ideas on teaching and learning did not penetrate into many departments (Tipton 1973). Many vocational teachers did not even see themselves as teachers but as subject specialists who happened to be in teaching (Gleeson and Mardle 1980).[4] As Venables comments in her study of colleges during the 1950s and 1960s, 'the nature of an institution inevitably affects the attitude of those who work in them and since colleges are not unequivocally educational institutions, members of staff do not, as a body see themselves consistently as educators' (1967: 220). One college principal described the majority of FE college teaching as:

suffering from being extremely pedestrian and uninspired with an unhealthy reliance on notes. There was a tendency for the teacher to lecture rather than teach. In other words he stood, or sat in front of the class and gave forth endlessly to a captive audience. In extreme cases he read straight from the textbook. There was no class participation; the students sat there mute, letting it wash over them.

(Bristow 1970: 53)

Although there were increases in the proportion of FE college teachers who were teacher-trained between 1944 and 1990, the culture of the 'old technical teacher' still maintained a strong presence in FE colleges of the early 1990s, particularly in vocational departments. Venables (1967) found that of the 250 teachers from nine technical colleges whom she interviewed, the overwhelming majority did not read any part of the educational press, but did read the technical publications concerned with their expertise. She commented that these teachers 'were concerned about the efficiency of their machinery but tended to accept that teaching methods and the examination system is unalterable' (Venables 1967: 139). Gleeson and Mardle (1980) found vocational teachers had very strong identities as trainers, not teachers. They identified with the backgrounds of their students and distanced themselves from those in other departments who had degrees and other qualifications associated with higher education. The approach of such teachers to their job was often found to be a reflection of their industrial socialisation:

hence classroom authority may be seen to be founded upon the fact that most teachers are recruited from industry, who have been through the system, and who are therefore well placed to pass on the know-how to those who also want their ticket. ... In both workshops and classrooms, the process of learning appears to be a highly formal affair, in which the teachers dictate or demonstrate particular principles or skills. ... Many teachers feel compelled to adopt a highly narrative and often didactic teaching style.

(Gleeson and Mardle 1980: 29)

As colleges broadened their student intake, new teaching and learning traditions were established which attracted new FE teachers and teachers from schools, and the proportion of those with teaching qualifications slowly increased (Cantor and Roberts 1986).[5] As FE colleges attracted more 16–19-year-olds in particular, a series of attempts took place to rationalise teacher training in the further and adult education sectors. The James Committee, set up by Margaret Thatcher when she was Secretary of State at the Department of Education and Science, reported in 1972 on the content and organisation of teacher training courses. While focusing primarily upon the school sector, for further education it proposed a 'three-cycle' system. The first phase was a two-year course in general education followed by a phase of initial teacher training which would continue into a third two-year phase of in-service training. The report simply assumed that a proportion of FE college teachers would come in at the second phase and that all full-time FE college teachers should have the same facilities as schoolteachers, particularly in the third in-service phase (DES 1972).

Although the more radical elements of the James Report were not developed, the general thrust of the report regarding increased opportunities for FE college teachers to be teacher-trained was broadly accepted (Foden 1992). In December 1972, the government issued a White Paper entitled *Education: a Framework for Expansion* (DES 1972a). This proposed an expansion of FE generally and an increase in teacher training for the sector. However, for a variety of complex reasons, partly related to the political and economic crisis of the early 1970s, and partly the low priority that FE has traditionally held with successive governments, these proposals were, once again, shelved.

Against this background, the Advisory Committee on the Supply and Training of Teachers (ACSETT) was established in October 1973. The first of three reports of a sub-committee of ACSETT was published in 1975 and became known as 'Haycocks 1' (DES 1975).[6] This report was concerned with the training of full-time FE teachers. It recommended that all new teachers who had not undergone initial training should undergo an induction course with an opportunity for a further year's release if they had less than three years' teaching experience. For established full-time staff, it recommended that a target of 5 per cent of full-time staff from any one college should at any one time be following a 'recognised' INSET day-release training course. The committee further recommended a system of national and regional councils to achieve co-ordination for the validation of the courses, and recommended that induction training be made compulsory by 1981.

The DES reacted favourably to Haycocks 1, and circular 11/77 (DES 1977) accepted the proposals in principle. However, because of restricted resources the DES lowered the target of 5 per cent of staff on INSET day-release at any one time to 3 per cent. The Department said it would reconsider the recommendations for compulsory induction only after the Regional Advisory Councils had made their next report in September 1978.

Haycocks 2 was published in 1978. This report was concerned with the training of part-time staff, who traditionally constituted a large and important part of the workforce in FE colleges.[7] At the time of the report (ACSETT 1978), very few part-time teachers in further education had a DES-recognised teacher qualification,[8] although some had the City and Guilds London Institute 730 qualification and some had the Royal Society of Arts or the College of Preceptors qualifications (Foden 1992). The report highlighted the fact that initial teacher training courses were not attracting many teachers with vocational qualifications and that the quality, criteria and comparability of ITE courses varied a great deal in the absence of the national regulatory body that had been recommended by Haycocks 1. The report recommended establishing a three-stage system to meet the needs of part-time teachers.

Although Haycocks 2 was not carried forward in detail, it did trigger an astonishing increase in part-time training, albeit on a voluntary basis. However, the majority of the increase in the training of part-time teachers was with those teaching in Adult Education Institutions, not FE colleges (Cantor and Roberts 1986).

Haycocks 3 was a discussion paper, *Training Teachers for Management in Further and Adult Education* (ACSETT 1978a). Having carried out a review of existing institutions, the paper concluded that the quality and quantity of FE college management could, and should, be improved. The vehicle for the improvements was the Regional Advisory Councils, which it proposed should make resources available for post initial in-service training. Little came of Haycocks 3 and its message was ignored; however, some training for senior management did take place during this period, but in an *ad hoc* and uncoordinated manner. The recommendation of Haycocks 2 for the induction training for all new staff by 1981 was never implemented.

Cantor and Roberts (1986) place great importance on the Haycocks reports, even though it was only Haycocks 1 that resulted in a DES circular. Of Haycocks 2 and Haycocks 3 Foden comments that 'both reports were remarkable: probably no government-sponsored body had ever before directed so much attention in such unfamiliar directions' (Foden 1992: 127). Although not fully implemented, the influence of these reports on the sector led to the proportion of trained teachers rising gradually throughout the 1970s and 1980s. Furthermore, the present provision of pre-service and in-service Certificate of Education/PGCEs owes much to the work of bodies such as the Regional Advisory Councils set up by Haycocks 1.

The period between 1944 and 1990 can be characterised as series of attempts by government-sponsored bodies to raise the issue of ITE and staff development in FE colleges. This greater interest in the quality of FE teaching coincided with the growing number of 16–19-year-olds in colleges following both general education courses and programmes catering for unemployed youth. However, attempts at improving the quality of FE provision, such as the James or Haycocks reports, were blocked or only accepted half-heartedly, then lost and forgotten as other more pressing priorities rose to the top of the government's educational agenda. A succession of government papers stressed the importance of higher levels of education and training in improving national competitiveness, but in the period between Haycocks 1 in 1975 and the early 1990s there was no clear policy concerning the quality of staff in the FE college sector (Guile and Lucas 1996). Instead, between 1944 and the early 1990s initial teacher education (ITE) and staff development for FE college teachers developed in an uneven manner. The quality of staff and their training was traditionally left for individual colleges and local education authorities to determine with no minimum qualifications required to teach in the FE college sector.[9] The result was that by 1990 initial teaching qualifications and the opportunities for professional development of staff continued to develop but still in an *ad hoc* way, much like the FE college sector in general (see chapter 1).

Initial training and further professional development prior to the incorporation of colleges in 1993

Until 1993, when FE colleges were incorporated, the governance and management of the FE sector lay in the hands of LEAs. No clear strategic leadership was provided by government departments or their national agencies. Arrangements for initial teacher education (ITE) and continuing professional development (CPD), or staff development as it was called in FE colleges, varied enormously between different teaching and learning traditions and throughout the further education college sector (Huddleston and Unwin 1997, 2002).[10] According to Cantor and Roberts (1986), many LEAs in the 1970s resisted sending teaching staff on courses because of the reluctance of colleges to release them from teaching duties. This confirms the view expressed by Castling (1996) that in the 1970s staff development mainly consisted of teachers being sent on a LEA-funded external courses to update them in their subject areas. In the 1980s, more emphasis was given to internal staff development as staff development funding became a more regulated, targeted activity with stated outcomes linked to strategic plans.

Before the incorporation of colleges in 1993, staff development was funded through the Department of Education and Science's (DES)[11] Grant for Educational Support and Training (GEST) budget,[12] which was overseen by LEAs (Cantor *et al.* 1995). GEST emerged from a series of initiatives designed to replace the *ad hoc* LEA funding of staff development. All of these initiatives were significant in as much as they represented the first attempt to regulate staff development programmes by laying down some national criteria, which earmarked funds for in-service training for teachers, replacing the past uneven approaches of LEA-funded staff development programmes.

Liaison over initial teacher education was conducted directly between

FE colleges and higher education institutions and was rarely subject to any systematic monitoring (Guile and Lucas 1996). Although an initial teaching qualification was accepted as desirable by many colleges and LEAs, there was little political or public concern about the actual nature or the uneven development of teacher training in the sector (Blackstone 1998). Thus, by the 1980s and 1990s, provision continued to be very uneven both in terms of the proportion of FE college teachers who held teacher qualifications, and the comparability and quality of the teacher training qualifications themselves (UPDC 1999). Some colleges continued with their existing arrangements for university-based ITE and their own pattern of provision for professional development (Lucas *et al.* 1996), while others embraced the National Council for Vocational Qualifications (NCVQ) competence-based approaches (Cantor *et al.* 1995). Although FE colleges and their teaching staff developed in a very uncoordinated manner, estimates of the number of FE college teachers who had a recognised teaching qualification in the early 1990s just prior to incorporation (discussed in chapter 2) was approximately 60 per cent to 70 per cent of full-time staff (Betts 1999).

Table 4.1 clearly indicates that the number of untrained teachers remained more or less stable from the mid-1970s and throughout the 1980s, but as the total number of FE college teachers grew they became a smaller proportion of the total. The number of qualified teachers in FE colleges rose steadily as academic and general vocational programmes expanded and as patterns of attendance shifted from part-time to more full-time courses (Cantor *et al.* 1995).[14] The growth of general education courses in FE colleges attracted many PGCE-qualified teachers from the secondary school sector and stimulated a growth in FE-focused initial training courses to cater for the new wave of FE college teachers who were less representative of industry and particular vocational areas. The number of qualified teachers continued to rise in the 1980s, and although DFE figures are not available for 1993/4, evidence suggests that the upward trend continued and certainly expanded in 1993 as a result of sixth-form colleges being included in the FE sector (Lucas and Betts 1996).[15] Furthermore, the DFE statistics show that slightly more women

Table 4.1 *Teacher qualifications of FE college teachers in England and Wales 1975–1991*[13]

Year	% of Graduates	Total staff	Trained in FE	Trained in HE	Untrained	% Trained
1975	41.5	49,469	11,171	9,935	28,363	**42.66**
1980	42.8	60,766	14,772	15,629	30,365	**50.02**
1985	46.1	64,117	16,970	17,476	29,671	**53.72**
1986		64,107	16,430	18,650	29,027	**53.88**
1987		65,101	15,968	20,091	29,042	**55.38**
1989		64,351	14,431	21,219	28,701	**55.39**
1990	48.2	56,124	12,749	18,826	24,545	**56.12**
1991	48.6	54,926	11,726	18,826	24,374	**55.62**

Table 4.1a *Male:Female ratio*

	1986	1989	1991
Men trained	52.44%	53.17%	54.20%
Women trained	60.19%	60.55%	58.45%

Source: Young *et al.* 1995: 23

than men have a teaching qualification, suggesting that there was little increase in the proportion of teacher qualified staff on vocational courses.[16]

The DFE awarded designated status[17] to nearly 40 universities and higher education colleges that provided Certificate of Education and PGCE teaching qualifications for those training to teach in FE colleges (NATFHE 1994). Of the 29 universities preparing teachers for employment in the FE sector, 19 were former polytechnics – an indication of the lack of engagement of the older universities with FE colleges in particular and vocational education and training in general. However, partly as a result of criteria introduced by Council for the Accreditation of Teacher Education (CATE), which allowed FE colleges to be used for teaching practice for secondary PGCE students, and partly out of an awareness that the FE college sector was expanding, a number of the 'old universities' began offering FE-focused ITE courses in the early 1990s (Hall

2000). It is difficult to measure the extent to which the pattern of those offering FE-focused ITE is changing. However, one pattern is clear. Until the 1980s, the further education teacher training centres at Huddersfield, Bolton, Wolverhampton and Garnett dominated higher education provision. During the 1990s provision of FE teacher training courses became more diversified across a much wider range of HE institutions (NATFHE 1994). Research of university ITE (FE) provision (UPDC 1999) found that some universities franchised the Certificate of Education out to FE colleges, whilst others had a partnership, with colleges offering part one of the course and universities offering part two. Some universities taught the whole ITE course, using FE colleges only for the student teacher to acquire teaching practice. The only common feature was the stress on practical teaching skills, but these were assessed quite differently.

The absence of any statutory requirement for FE college teachers to obtain an initial teaching qualification and the absence of any national quality assurance body, such as CATE or the TTA for school ITE, also resulted in a multiplicity of arrangements for accreditation towards the Certificate of Education and PGCE. A report for the Association for Colleges in 1995 raised doubts about the comparability, quality and value of many ITE courses and staff development qualifications (Young *et al.* 1995). Furthermore, UPDC (1999) research found little common practice between ITE courses when it came to the minimum and maximum amount of teaching hours to be undertaken by full-time pre-service student teachers for their teaching practice in colleges. Some universities specified the amount of hours to be undertaken on teaching practice, although this varied; others did not specify at all. The same unevenness applied to the number of supervised teaching visits from tutors from universities while teaching practice was undertaken in the FE college.

As well as the Certificate of Education and PGCEs available to FE college teachers, there was also a range of other qualifications outside DFE-designated courses. These qualifications, such as the City and Guilds 7307, were mainly offered by FE colleges and other training providers, rather than by higher education institutions. Reliable figures of the number of teachers undertaking these other qualifications are not available.

The number of FE colleges offering City and Guilds teaching certificates within FE colleges was estimated in the early 1990s to be 250 of the 450 FE colleges in the sector (NATFHE 1994).[18] City and Guilds awarded 730 series certificates to over 10,000 candidates in 1992/3, although they estimated that a quarter of these were for trainers outside the FE college sector (Young *et al.* 1995), illustrating again the diversity of the FE sector, the *ad hoc* nature of teaching qualifications and the entrepreneurial approach of the awarding bodies (Peeke and Spencer 1998).

Conclusion

This chapter has examined the development of teacher education and the professional development of further education teachers from the late nineteenth century up to FE incorporation in 1993. In general, teacher education and professional development for the FE sector is a history of 'benign neglect', with both the state and teachers themselves assuming that vocational or subject expertise was a sufficient qualification to teach in FE colleges (Robson 1998). This legacy produced a culture in FE where many teachers' identity was primarily tied to their expertise, resulting in diverse and fragmented professional practices. Despite FE colleges becoming more diverse institutions from the 1970s, the professional practice of FE teachers was not influenced by new ideas or broader debates concerning teaching and learning, and often the FE teachers' professional practice remained isolated within their specialism. This in turn reinforced the diverse and divided teaching and learning cultures and acted as a barrier to the development of a sense of collective professional values and standards among FE teachers.

Although efforts were made to regulate and fund staff development programmes in the 1980s, as FE entered incorporation in 1993 there was still no statutory requirement for teaching qualifications and no minimum qualifications at all for those who taught in the FE sector. The qualifications and quality of FE college teachers was left for LEAs and individual colleges to decide. While there was a steady increase in FE teachers with teaching qualifications between 1944 and 1993, initial teacher education and staff development programmes developed in a fragmented and unplanned way, raising concerns about the quality and comparability of Certificate of Education and PGCE courses and the multiplicity of arrangements in colleges and HEIs. This diverse and uneven situation is the starting point of the next chapter, which traces the development of initial teacher education and professional development of FE teachers from 1993 when colleges entered incorporation.

Notes

1 By the mid-twentieth century many of what are now FE colleges were known as technical colleges. In the historical account they shall be called 'technical colleges' until the 1960s and then the term FE colleges will be used.
2 See chapter 8.
3 As outlined in chapter 9 this confusion between the roles and functions of a teacher, instructor, assessor, trainer and learning support worker still exists within the sector today and poses challenges for staff development and ITE.
4 They called themselves lecturers.
5 See chapters 1 and 8.
6 All three reports were named after the Chair, Norman Haycocks.
7 The report also concerned itself with adult education not provided in further education colleges. In adult education part-time teachers often constituted a large majority carrying most of the teaching load.
8 This was a PGCE or a Certificate of Education.
9 Some colleges did insist that all full-time staff achieve a teacher qualification as part of the contract of employment (Lucas *et al.* 1996).
10 For example, academic programmes such as A levels attracted teachers from schools who were teacher-trained.
11 The DES was replaced by the Department for Education (DfE) in 1992.
12 GEST emerged from a scheme called TVEI Related In-Service Initiative (TRIST).
13 This is based upon research that looked at DfE Statistics of Education. It does not include part-time AEI staff. The DfE statistics did not specify which teacher qualifications they counted or whether their statistics included teachers in polytechnics.
14 See chapters 1 and 3.

15 The incorporation of sixth-form colleges into the FE sector is discussed in chapter 2.
16 This could reflect the male domination of traditional vocational courses.
17 Designation by the DfE (now DfES) means that courses receive mandatory awards such as fees.
18 The City and Guilds 730 series was by far the most popular non-DfEE recognised qualification.

5 Teacher education and staff development 1993–1999

The deployment of teachers and the increase in part-time staff

An FEFC inspection report in 1999 entitled *Professional Development in Further Education* pointed to a lack of investment in staff development by a 'sector that should be convinced of the benefits of training' (FEFC 1999: 22). The report confirmed previous research that showed that there had been a large increase in the proportion of part-time teaching staff in FE colleges. A contemporary estimate of the effects of incorporation had showed that in the previous five years 20,000 permanent jobs had been lost, while at the same time there had been an estimated 33-per-cent increase in student numbers (Betts 1999). These job losses have affected some departments more than others, with the losses concentrated on areas such as engineering (Ainley and Bailey 1997) and middle management (*FE Now!* 1997). On the other hand, growth in the number of full-time staff has been recorded in programme areas such as travel and tourism, business studies, IT courses and media studies (Hill 2000).

While it is hard to get an accurate picture of staff changes, evidence firmly indicates that there had been a drop in full-time staff and an increase in part-time posts. It has been estimated that colleges were spending around 30 per cent of their staffing budgets on part-time staff, although this statistic hides a huge variation in local practice (McGavin 1998). Research by Betts (1999) suggested that the proportion of part-time staff per college was on average 66 per cent within a range of 1 per cent to 92 per cent. This increase in part-time posts was matched by the growing use of temporary staff in general (Mackney 1998), which in turn not only raised the levels of job insecurity but also had implications for the quality of teaching and learning. The proportion of full-time to part-time staff in 1997 was 38 per cent and 62 per cent respectively, with Betts

(1999) suggesting that part-time staff delivered half of the FE college curriculum.

Table 5.1 *Full-time and part-time staff in FE colleges in 1997*

Teach full-time	43,400	38% of teaching staff
Teach part-time	71,900	62% of teaching staff
Support staff full-time	10,900	52% of support staff
Support staff part-time	10,300	48% of support staff
Other full-time	30,700	55%
Other part-time	25,100	45%

Source: FEFC 1999b based upon SIR July 1997 from 385 colleges

The important issue for the purposes of this chapter is not just the growth in the proportion of part-time staff, but the fact that most colleges did not provide staff development to part-time staff and 'there were few opportunities for part-time staff to participate in curriculum development or work with other teachers in teams' (FEFC 1999b: 23). Many colleges simply did not provide staff development for part-time staff if they were employed for less than a certain number of hours, often between 8 and 10 hours per week (FEFC 1996). The FEFC Chief Inspector's report stated that the apparent lack of training opportunities for part-time staff was serious because 'part-time staff (who in some colleges do as much as 50 per cent of the teaching) ... rarely engage in curriculum development, student support and guidance activities, extra curriculum provision, formal staff appraisal and in-service training' (FEFC 1996: 6).

Alongside the increased use of part-time staff already mentioned above, there was a blurring of the distinction between teaching and non-teaching staff when 'instructor' or 'assessor' grades were introduced into FE colleges. Evidence suggested that the introduction of some 'instructor grades' with just TDLB assessor qualifications (AoC 1999) was a further move towards a fragmented workforce, typically reflected in the division between the academic and vocational curriculum (Gee 1997). This development was matched by a shift in salary bands, with teaching posts in some FE colleges advertised in 1998 not from a wide band as in pre-incorporation arrangement, but divided into a number of new categories with much narrower salary bands and separate job descriptions (Williams 1998). A new type of support tutor was being introduced into colleges with responsibility for recording prior learning and achievement and providing self-study support to students (Huddleston and Unwin 1997). These developments, which were not in themselves detrimental to teaching staff, and could be seen as positive developments (Withers 1998), took place within the context of the loss of full-time jobs and the absence of staff development programmes (Lumby and Tomlinson 2000), and this allowed staff to develop and move between the new categories that were being introduced, thereby fragmenting FE colleges' staff still further (Lucas and Betts 1996).[1]

Another example of the increased fragmentation of FE college staff during these years was the growing use of agency staff for teaching. Education Lecturing Services (ELS 1996) claimed in their promotional material that a number of colleges have a human resource strategy made up of a 'tight core' of full- and part-time staff and a 'non-core', contract part-time staff. ELS demonstrated how 'on costs' could be reduced by adopting a core/non-core approach to staffing (Randle and Bradey 1997). Colleges using agency staff claimed this increased the job security and development for their core staff. This was done by using non-core agency staff to reduce redundancy consultation, removing possible claims for unfair dismissal and claims under equal opportunity legislation, because many non-core part-time staff are women (ELS 1996).

The increasing use of part-time staff, the use of employment agencies and the division of teachers into different salary bands, as outlined above, all illustrate the extent to which further fragmentation among FE college teachers developed during the mid-1990s (Guile and Lucas 1999). This is reflected in FEFC reports such as *Quality and Standards in Further Education in England* (1996), which claimed that funding and financial considerations, rather than educational ones, were dominating the debate in FE colleges, and that fears of redundancy were sapping staff morale: 'such changes in relation to staffing are not always in the best interests of students' (FEFC 1996: 6).

The implications of all these developments are quite complex and have had long-term effects. The blurring of roles and the creation of new divisions between staff may well be an appropriate response to a more flexible curriculum and to changing teaching and learning patterns in FE colleges (Lucas and Betts 1996). *FE Now!* claimed that an East Birmingham college had very low costs because 'of the cost efficiency of the Charles Handy model, with one third permanent staff, one third agency staff and one third portfolio workers' (*FE Now!* 1997: 9). Charles Handy's (1989) model of organisation uses the image of a shamrock for three key segments in the workforce. The core segment consists of well qualified professionals who work hard and long but who receive substantial rewards both in terms of salary and career. The second segment consists of a contractual fringe made up of self-employed professionals or technicians, in groups or as individuals, who are paid fees based on completing defined tasks. The third leaf Handy calls the flexible labour force. These are people who are used when required on part-time or short-term contracts of employment (Scott 2001). Some members of the flexible labour force may be part-time or temporary by choice, but most will have no choice. Handy also mentions a fourth leaf (thereby destroying his analogy of a shamrock), which consists of the growing tendency towards 'self-service', where customers help themselves.

The model of organisation described by Handy can be used to help make some sense of structural change and the new patterns of staff deployment in FE colleges since incorporation. What the model highlights is the way in which such an approach to human resource management seeks flexibility by increasing the division of labour. FE has always had a 'core' and 'periphery', although since incorporation the 'contractual fringe' and 'flexible labour force' have grown. In other words, employers were seeking flexibility by adopting new and particular human resource management (HRM) strategies (Elliott 1997). Another approach would be to put more emphasis on developing and empowering the individual to work in new and more flexible ways, through human resource development (HRD). HRM is a concept from business rather than from education and was used in FE colleges to meet the system demands of the FEFC. It emphasises managing people to perform to results rather than to educational or pedagogic strategies (Holloway 1999). HRD on the other hand, is part of a strategic approach to developing people in organisations to prepare for the future (Randle and Bradey 1998). The distinction between the two approaches to human resources can become blurred because both took place in colleges during this period. For example, with the growth of part-time teachers and a greater division of labour more responsibility was taken on by existing full-time teaching staff, such as curriculum management and development. While the expansion of student numbers in FE colleges was not solely caused by incorporation, the expansion during this period further increased the diversity of learning needs, leading to pressure for curriculum change and innovation (Withers 1998). Furthermore, pressures not attributable to incorporation, such as changes in information and computer technology and other structural, economic and technological developments, also brought about contradictory pressures for change in the professional practice of FE college teachers (Avis 1999). According to Huddleston and Unwin (2002), the new roles full-time teaching staff are being expected to undertake in FE colleges include counselling students, marketing and promoting their own courses, managing budgets and course teams, and developing open and flexible learning systems as well as new learning techniques for distance and independent learning. Therefore, while there has been a growth of diversity and fragmentation within the professional practice of FE teachers since incorporation, there are also many pressures that demand a broader professional practice.

Staff development and initial teacher education 1993–1997

In introducing the incorporation of colleges, the Conservative government severed the link between colleges, LEAs and national funding for staff development (Spours and Lucas 1996). The new Further Education

Funding Council (FEFC) assumed that decisions about the level of investment in continuing professional development were the responsibility of individual colleges and not the FEFC's concern (Cantor *et al.* 1995). There was no body with responsibility for the quality of initial training of FE college teachers equivalent to the now defunct Council for the Accreditation of Teacher Education (CATE), which accredited initial teacher training courses for schoolteachers, or its successor the Teacher Training Agency (TTA) (Lucas 1996). The arrangements for initial teacher education (ITE) and professional development developed in an even more fragmented way during incorporation, as both became based on the individual policies of the 460 or so incorporated colleges (Ollin 1996). In the absence of any coherent plan for the FE sector, an unevenness developed in the value, quality and comparability of ITE and staff development courses offered by HE institutions and FE.

Despite the unevenness, evidence suggests that the actual number of untrained teachers remained more or less stable from the mid-1970s to the end of the 1980s, but became a smaller proportion of the total FE teaching staff as the number of new, teacher-qualified, full-time staff increased. Furthermore, although DfE figures are not available for 1993/4, evidence suggested that the upward trend continued and certainly expanded in 1993 as a result of sixth-form colleges being included in the FE sector (Lucas and Betts 1996) following incorporation.

After this expansion in the period to 1993, however, the proportion of teacher-trained FE teachers declined. An FEFC report (1999b) expressed concern about changes to staff development programmes since incorporation, suggesting that colleges had responded to immediate demands made upon teaching staff by the FEFC and other immediate needs such as gaining TDLB assessor awards. Very few colleges had 'given priority to the development of effective teaching skills even when lesson inspection grades reveal pedagogic weakness' (FEFC 1999b: 7).[2] Earlier the FEFC had commented that in many inspection reports poor teaching in FE colleges was mainly seen as a consequence of insufficient knowledge by teachers of how learning takes place, particularly within the context of the growing diversity of students (FEFC 1996).

Furthermore, the FEFC pointed to weaknesses in staff development programmes, including:

> the relatively low levels of finance allocated to staff development, in a sector that should believe in the benefits of training; insufficient analysis of the costs and benefits of staff development activities; the shortage of sufficient opportunities for industrial and professional updating; the low priority given to pedagogic skills, in comparison to assessor training; and insufficient opportunities to prepare for curriculum change.

(FEFC 1999b: 1).[3]

Drawing fully reliable comparisons between the statistics produced by the DfE up to 1991 and the FEFC data produced in 1996/7 is rather difficult. This is because the DfE only counted full-time staff attaining DfE-designated ITE courses, such as the PGCE and the Certificate of Education, while the FEFC counted non-DfEE-recognised ITE qualifications such as BSc. Table 5.2 presents FEFC data for the qualifications of teachers in FE colleges in 1996/7.

Table 5.2 *FEFC data on highest qualifications of FE college teachers 1996/7*

Mode	Highest level of teacher training qualification attained									
	BEd/BA/ BSc	Certificate of Education	PGCE	C&G 730	TDLB	Other	None	Not known	Total	Distribution %
Full-time	8,000	13,400	8,300	3,200	1,600	1,600	4,100	3,300	43,400	38
Part-time	5,600	7,800	4,700	6,900	1,400	4,600	9,800	31,100	71,900	62
% of known	17	26	16	12	4	8	17			

Source: FEFC (1999b) Staff Individualised Record Data, 31 July 1997 (1996/7)
Coverage: 385 colleges
Note: Data are rounded to the nearest 100

However, by comparing the data from the FEFC and estimates from 1993, table 5.3 illustrates the sweeping changes in the proportion of part-time to full-time teaching staff in the first four years of incorporation.

The significance of the drift towards more part-time staff is that the FEFC estimated that while 68 per cent of full-time teachers were teacher-

Table 5.3 *Numbers and percentage of part-time and full-time FE college teachers between 1993/4 and 1996/7*

	1993/4	% of total	1996/7	% of total
Full-time	51,000	51%	43,400	38%
Part-time	49,000	49%	71,900	62%

Sources: Young *et al.* 1995; Bell 1996; FEFC 1999b; DfEE 2000a

trained, only 25 per cent of part-time teachers had full teaching qualifications. Table 5.4 applies this estimate by the FEFC to available data on FE teachers in 1993/4. By adding part-time and full-time staff together, the calculation suggests that because of the growth of the proportion of part-time to full-time teaching, the total number of FE teachers possessing full DFE recognised teaching qualifications fell in this first period of incorporation, reversing the trend of the past two decades.

Table 5.4 *Numbers and percentage of FE college teachers with DfE/DfEE initial teaching qualifications between 1993/4 and 1996/7*

	1993/4		1996/7	
	All	With ITE	All	With ITE
Full-time[4]	51,000	34,680	43,400	28,512
Part-time[5]	49,000	12,250	71,900	17,975
Total	100,000	46,930	115,300	46,487
ITE qualifications		*46.9%*		*40.3%*

Sources: Young *et al.* 1995; Bell 1996; FEFC 1999b; DfEE 2000a

The evidence that the proportion of FE teachers with initial teaching qualifications declined after incorporation between 1993 and 1999 is matched by evidence that staff development programmes followed a similar pattern. As colleges entered incorporation, it was estimated by Young *et al.* (1995) that the level of targeted funding for staff development was between 1 and 3 per cent of FE college income. However, in 1999 the FEFC estimated that in 1998 the average expenditure on staff development was within an overall range of between 0.15 per cent and just above 2.00 per cent of a college's income (FEFC 1999b).[6] There is also evidence to suggest that a large proportion of money allocated to staff development was spent on enabling college managers to receive training on Management Information Systems (MIS), Individual Student Records (ISR) and other immediate aspects of administration arising from the data demands of the FEFC (Lucas *et al.* 1999). As the FEFC points out, very little of the staff development budget was spent on curriculum development, improving teaching techniques, or developing strategies to help students learn. The exception seems to be those teachers working specifically with students with recognised learning difficulties (FEFC 1999b).

While pointing to many weaknesses, the FEFC report does praise some staff development schemes and systems, and the relatively high proportion of staff with teaching qualifications in a sector where they are not a compulsory requirement. In particular, the report draws attention to the fact that 92 per cent of teachers stated that they used FEFC inspection reports to identify good practice.

There is evidence of teaching qualifications being valued by FE staff. In a sample survey of 687 full-time FE staff it was found that 72.7 per cent wanted some form of Qualified Teacher Status (QTS) to be introduced for FE college teachers, and 82 per cent agreed that a probationary year should be served by full-time teaching staff, with 76.7 per cent feeling that a Certificate of Education should be achieved during that period (Hill 2000). When asked, 81.1 per cent of FE college teachers believed it was important that they were considered to be members of the teaching profession and 78.6 per cent wanted to be part of a General Teaching Council, with only 3.9 per cent disagreeing. This reflects the FEFC's finding (1999b) of progress towards the acceptance of national standards and mandatory qualifications for FE college teachers and managers, as well as that of earlier research (Peeke 1999) that revealed a more positive attitude towards teaching qualifications for all FE college teachers.

Conclusion

During incorporation between 1993 and 1999 existing pre-incorporation divisions between FE teachers were exacerbated. There was an increased use of part-time and agency teachers, and the loss of full-time, experienced FE staff. The introduction of a range of different teaching grades with different functions, pay bands and job descriptions further blurred the division between teaching and support staff.

Incorporation also saw a decrease in the proportion of FE college teachers with DfE/DfEE recognised initial teaching qualifications. Despite growing student diversity and increased demands on teachers, staff development programmes also declined as a proportion of FE college budgets between 1993 and 1997.

Paradoxically during the same period there was a growing concern about the quality of teaching and the professional practice of staff, reflecting FE's growing role in raising skill levels and promoting lifelong learning. As a consequence of the growing importance of the FE sector, FE teachers were subject to greater regulation in the form of a national inspection regime, a national funding formula and a range of national performance indicators.

Notes

1 It is not suggested that incorporation has deprofessionalised the FE college teacher (Randle and Bradey 1997). There has never been a collective or identifiable set of professional values and practices in FE. The argument is that the practice of FE college teachers has become more fragmented.
2 See chapter 2.
3 The FEFC also suggested that ITE courses for the sector have 'less preparation for the teaching of specific subjects or disciplines than in the past' (FEFC 1999b: 18).
4 Calculated at FEFC estimate that 68 per cent of full-time teachers have ITE qualifications.
5 Calculated at FEFC estimate that 25 per cent of part-time teachers have ITE qualifications.
6 This is taken from 108 FEFC inspections between September 1997 and May 1998.

6 Growing regulation: standards or standardisation?

The momentum towards identifying the competencies needed by FE college teachers increased during the early 1990s as the approach to competence promoted by the National Council for Vocational Qualifications (NCVQ) embedded itself in FE colleges. An important development along the path towards an NVQ model of initial training and staff development for FE college staff was the establishment of the Training and Development Lead Body (TDLB) in 1990. Its purpose was to develop standards applied to training and development in all sectors of employment (FEU 1992).

Initially, the TDLB standards were devised to address the instruction and supervision of training in companies (Chown 1992), and aimed to address the need to standardise the assessment of NVQs. However, the TDLB also developed a range of competencies to cover teaching, assessing, management roles and staff development in the FE sector. During the mid to late 1990s, TDLB standards had a considerable impact on FE college staff because of the major Awarding Bodies' 'Common Accord', which agreed a common set of practices for NVQ assessment. The Accord was strongly backed by the NCVQ and it became a requirement that all teachers on NVQs and GNVQs achieve TDLB Assessor Awards, which were then substituted for, or accredited towards, whole qualifications.[1] As part of the process of placing the awards within an NVQ framework, standards were broken down into key roles, units, elements, range indicators, performance and assessment criteria (Ecclestone 1997). These awards had an immediate impact on college staff training priorities, reflecting a more general trend towards competence-based approaches, which explicitly or implicitly led to training provision being replaced by a process of verification and certification of existing competencies (Hyland 1995).

The Further Education Unit (FEU) trialled and promoted the TDLB standards alongside Management Charter Initiative (MCI) standards.[2] This, in effect, was a move away from professional qualifications being legitimated by higher education to an NCVQ-based model (Garland 1993). The FEU held seminars to discuss, 'what would be needed to be added to the TDLB standards in order to meet the requirements of the Cert. Ed (FE) as a professional development qualification?' (FEU 1994: 1). Some universities wanted the standards to make explicit all that is implied by the idea of a teacher as a 'reflective practitioner',[3] whilst others wished to incorporate MCI and TDLB standards as they stood into existing ITE and professional development programmes. A number of 'new' universities approached the NCVQ to ask if universities could go to the NCVQ for 'kite marking' (FEU 1994a).[4] Some universities devised in-house competency-based programmes and the Universities Professional Development Consortium (UPDC) was set up to accredit TDLB standards as part of university-based programmes,[5] where some of the units of the TDLB awards were integrated into existing university initial teacher training programmes. Many universities had redesigned their ITE courses on the NCVQ/TDLB model, even calling for 'product evidence' in their assessment in order to conform to NVQ criteria (Maynard 1995). A survey in 1997/8 showed that all 39 universities and colleges in the survey were working with some form of competence-based assessment. Fifty per cent of those surveyed were completely competence-based and 67 per cent of those universities questioned had incorporated or intended to incorporate TDLB units into their provision (University of Wolverhampton 1998).

Functional mapping and the staff development forum

The momentum to apply NVQs to FE teacher training and professional development was pushed one step further in 1994, when the DFE and Employment Department decided to develop a higher level NVQ for FE college teachers. In 1995, it was decided to produce a 'functional map' of the FE college sector 'to help inform Ministers making decisions on whether there should be a lead body for the FE college sector or some other arrangement' (DfEE/FEDA 1995: 5). The project was initially managed by the FEU, and then by its successor body, the Further Education Development Agency (FEDA). FEDA was empowered to establish a staff development forum to develop national teaching standards and form an embryo lead body for the FE college sector. It was decided by the DfEE to hire consultants, to take the 'functional mapping' forward. The objectives were to:

> Prepare an occupational map identifying the number, job titles, qualifications and development programmes for those in the sector; secondly, building on the occupational map and consultation with the sector, prepare a functional map which developed an initial functional analysis of the sector to a stage which enables both the recognition by the sector of occupational roles and comparisons with other sectors.
>
> (DfEE/FEDA 1995: 5)

The purpose of the functional map was agreed with the NCVQ and SCOTVEC (Scottish Vocational Education Council). Its aim was to express outcomes, results and achievements rather than activities, tasks and underpinning knowledge or any other requirement which might be attributed to individuals. From these key roles it was proposed by the DfEE and FEDA that units of competence could be developed in order to make them conform to NVQs and SVQs. The result of the mapping produced a thick volume of maps and charts, illustrating a bewildering array of diversity. In trying to analyse job titles under the heading 'teaching and learning', 56 different titles were identified. This was from a grand total of 193 different job titles used in the FE college sector.

Starting from one key purpose, four domains were identified; from the domains, 19 key areas emerged, which were then broken down into 67 key roles. These key roles formed the base upon which units of competence could be developed, presumably to meet the 193 job titles. Each key role was then mapped against standards set by 40 lead bodies, occupational standards councils, or industry training organisations, which were relevant to further education and the approximately 40 full NVQs and SVQs that these bodies offered. The ultimate logic of skills mapping appeared not only to lead to a most complicated and bureaucratic system, designed to place initial teacher training and further professional development within an NVQ framework, it also seemed that gaining a teaching qualification would become a process of verification of work-based skills. In order to take the mapping exercise and the report forward the DfEE established the Further Education Staff Development Forum (FESDF) in 1996. The brief of the FESDF was to arrive at a set of national standards for all occupations in the FE college sector, to liaise with other standard-setting bodies and to develop a framework for initial training and professional development for FE college teachers (Peeke 1999). Although the establishment of the FESDF was seen by some as the precursor of an employer lead body for FE (Guile and Lucas 1996), the composition of the FESDF had a broader representation than most lead bodies, since it included professional associations, unions and local government (FESDF 1997).[6] The FESDF tackled the development of the functional map, citing the *Draft National Guidelines on Provision Leading to the Teaching Qualification (FE) and Related Professional Development* (SOEID 1997) as a possible model for the future.[7] There was, however, no clear consensus among members of the Forum that England and Wales should adopt the Scottish approach, which involved adopting a narrow competence-based approach and NVQ framework for the training of their FE teachers (FESDF 1997a).

Initially, the majority of the members of the FESDF adopted a positive attitude to the Scottish standards, noting that they drew on the TDLB model. A significant minority opposed teacher education becoming narrowly competence-based. The FESDF Standards Sub-group was presented with the SOIED guidelines, which consisted of units and outcomes (FESDF 1997b). The Awarding Bodies Sub-group was, in the meantime, invited to map existing FE college teacher qualifications against the functional map of the FE college sector produced by some consultants (FESDF 1997a). Another group of consultants was hired to consult FE colleges about the standards. At a Staff Development Forum workshop in October 1997, the FE 'standards' were presented to a select group chosen by FEDA for initial discussion prior to taking them to colleges. In the document presented to the group, the word 'standards' had been replaced by 'competencies', expressed in terms of units, elements, indicators of competence, knowledge specification and personal competencies (Forum 1997). It seemed as though the word standards was used interchangeably with competences and meant the same thing (Armitage *et al.* 2003).

Consultation: from competence to national standards

During consultations with colleges in 1997, a clear change in the nature of the debate took place, as meeting after meeting confirmed the view that colleges did not want TDLB- or NCVQ-type competencies. Further education college staff, when consulted, wanted a holistic approach with broad standards that allowed for professional judgement and knowledge (Peeke 1999). In his report to the QCA, Dr Peeke described the workshops and consultation meetings as 'a lively affair' with strong opinions being voiced about avoiding the 'functional approach to standards', which was still closely associated with competence. The consultation confirmed that competence and TDLB qualifications had a poor image among FE college staff, who saw them as inappropriate for recognising teachers' professionalism (UCET 1999b).

A clear message for the consultants and members of the Staff Development Forum to consider came out of the extensive consultation.[8] Further education college teachers, while welcoming the move towards professional standards, did not want them expressed in functional terms (FEDA 1999b). They wanted broad statements that could allow for professional interpretation and reflective practice (FEDA 1999a). Further education college teachers also said in the consultation meetings that they wanted a clear rationale for the structure of the standards and a section on the values of teaching in FE colleges. Furthermore, the rationale and statement of values should reflect FE's diversity and the centrality of teacher professionalism (Peeke 1999). As a result of this feedback, a third draft went out for consultation in which the narrow competence approach was replaced by a much broader interpretation of the standards. This draft took the views expressed at the consultation meetings into account and the FE standards were shifted from a narrow interpretation of competencies for an NVQ framework back to a broad interpretation of professional standards. Further drafts were produced from a series of focus groups and regional workshops held in early 1998. From the focus groups and workshops, another draft was produced and this was trialled in ten institutions. The results of the trial were reported on 24 July 1998 (FEDA 1999) and informed the final draft of the standards. In all, the process had involved 238 colleges, 10 HE institutions and 23 other agencies and organisations. The FESDA standards were launched with the new Further Education National Training Organisation (FENTO) in January 1999 and became the FENTO standards outlined in table 6.1.

Table 6.1 *FENTO standards*

Meet professional requirements		
• work within a professional value base		
• conform to agreed code of professional conduct		
Professional knowledge	**Key areas of teaching**	**Personal skills and attributes**
• the place of FE in the wider context	• planning and preparing teaching and learning programmes for groups and individuals	• critical self-reflection
• knowledge of subject area		• effective communication with groups and individuals
• learning theory, teaching approaches and methodologies	• developing and using a range of teaching and learning techniques	• integrity, reliability and confidence
• effects of change on the FE sector and teachers' practice	• managing the learning process	• empathy, rapport and respect for learners and colleagues
	• providing learners with support	
	• assessing the outcomes of learners and learners' achievements	
	• reflecting upon and evaluating one's own performance and planning future needs	
	• assessing learners' needs	

New Labour policy: National Training Organisations and FENTO

In essence, the Labour government elected in May 1997 continued the Conservative administration's policies of putting employers in control of standards (DE/DES 1986). Such an approach was based upon the belief that putting employers in overall control of standard-setting bodies would raise skills and standards in industrial training without the government taking any direct responsibility (Hodgson and Spours 1999). This approach led to the development of sector-specific 'Lead Industry Bodies' (LIBs) in the late 1980s, 160 of which were eventually established. The LIBs were given the responsibility for designing occupational standards of competence upon which NVQs could be based.

By the mid-1990s, it became a widely held view that the 160 lead bodies had generated confusion and overlap and that a more strategic approach was required (CBI 1994). In April 1996, the government initiated an attempt to rationalise the system by introducing new sectional National Training Organisations (NTOs), which would have a more strategic role and would replace the Lead Industry Bodies and Industry Training Organisations (ITOs). These NTOs were, according to the government, a rationalisation of the old Lead Industry Bodies and would encourage employers to express a greater interest in, and commitment to, the training and development of their staff, thus de-emphasising the government's own role in promoting training and development within UK industry (DfEE 1998a).[9]

NTOs were a central part of the Labour government's strategy for improving training. According to the NTO National Council (NTONC), NTOs represent 'a new era for training in Britain because they will spearhead the development of skills by working with employers to increase the uptake of NVQs and SVQs which are based upon them' (NTONC 1999: 1). Given the NTOs' role in defining national occupational standards, they were expected to implement their own and other S/NVQs and advise on the qualifications framework for their sectors (DfEE 1998a).[10] NTOs were principally employer-led bodies, which represented employers' interests in relation to the national skills agenda (DfEE 1998a). Indeed, according to the NTOs' employer guide, NTOs were 'owned and led by employers' (NTONC 1999).

The Secretary of State for Education and Employment approved the establishment of an NTO for FE (FENTO) in late 1998. The standards adopted by FENTO were officially launched in January 1999 and a Chief Executive was appointed and took up his post in October 1999. The composition of FENTO was dominated by employers, with some representation from the four nations, major FE organisations, governors and trade unions. The details of FENTO's budget were not described, although the DfEE stated that it would need to be self-financing within three years.

Different NTOs were also being set up, adding layers to an already complicated education and training scenario (Raggatt and Williams 1999) and it seems that different NTOs are working in their own ways without as yet, any co-ordination between them. According to Coffield (1992), this is predictable since the dependence on employers encourages the development of more market-orientated, narrow task-based NVQs built upon short-term needs rather than on long-term strategic planning. Alongside FENTO there were also separate NTOs for Adult and Community Education and Youth Work,[11] as well as other NTOs such as Local Government, Science, Technology and Mathematics (a cross-sector employment NTO), Higher Education and Training and many others. All NTOs are co-ordinated by the Board of the National Council of NTOs made up of senior employers.

There were concerns that the proliferation of NTOs could result in FE college teachers working to different standards set by different NTOs (Lucas 2000). Unlike FENTO, most NTOs develop NVQs, which are supervised by the QCA, while many teacher training qualifications are provided at HE level, which falls outside the remit of the QCA (FEDA 1999). Furthermore, the government strategy that led to a myriad of NTOs with a relationship to the FE college sector was likely to perpetuate the fragmentation of post-16 education and training and would not reinforce the possibility of a more strategic approach to these issues.

How NTOs were going to work with the new Learning and Skills

Councils (see chapters 3 and 7) was never made clear. All of the NTOs, with the exception of FENTO, were working to enhance NVQs and GNVQs. FENTO itself remained quite different from other NTOs and remained committed to working in an inclusive manner by, for example, including trade union representation in its national committees. It also moved away from adopting a narrow NVQ approach to teaching standards. However, like all NTOs, FENTO had low levels of funding and very few staff. Anecdotal evidence also suggested that the attendance of employers at FENTO meetings was very poor, which indicates that FE college employers were giving the development low priority.

A further complication was the relationship between FENTO, the Institute for Learning and Teaching (ILT) in Higher Education and the Teacher Training Agency (TTA), each of which adopted a different approach to standards. Yet these bodies were charged with ensuring that the arrangements did not prevent teachers crossing the different education sectors. There was also the question of the relationship between the Adult Learning Inspectorate (ALI) and OFSTED, which was responsible for inspecting provision for 16–19-year-olds in colleges as well as ITE programmes in universities. This raises interesting issues concerning how the two inspectorates, OFSTED and ALI, were going to approach the FENTO standards and how the different inspection criteria and traditions of OFSTED and the FEFC inspectorate were going to work together (see chapter 7 for the OFSTED report on the FENTO standards).

How FENTO and other standard setters in the FE sector were intending to co-ordinate with the new inspection regimes was never clear. Furthermore, not only were there many NTOs, but they were also UK-wide, spanning, in the case of FE colleges, quite different traditions and standards in FE colleges in Scotland and Northern Ireland. How NTOs were going to fit into devolved government and regional planning was never made clear. FENTO's strategy was to create four National FENTO Committees, thus side-stepping the difficulty of Scotland, Wales and Northern Ireland wishing to work to their own standards, in their own way.

Concern was been expressed that the government was treating FE teachers differently from all the other sectors of education (Dee 1999).

Primary and secondary teachers had the General Teaching Council (GTC), while teachers in higher education had an Institute for Learning and Teaching. Both of these bodies stressed the professional nature of teaching. FE colleges, alone among education institutions, had an employer-led body, FENTO (see chapter 7 for the present position under the Sector Skills Council). This blurred the important distinction between professional concerns and employer concerns (Hoyle and John 1995) that is recognised in most other professions as well as in the school and university sectors. On the other hand, FENTO, the teachers unions and others have attempted to establish a professional body for FE college teachers called the Institute for Learning. This held its first meeting in June 2003 (IfL 2003). However, as yet very few FE college teachers know of this body and there is as yet little or no incentive for FE college teachers to join.

Despite these areas of uncertainty, the standards have been broadly welcomed by those concerned about the professional practice of FE teachers (UCET 1999), not only because of the move away from competence-based approaches such as those being used in Scotland (mentioned above), but also because, with all their faults, the standards represent a first historic attempt to arrive at national standards for FE college teachers (Nash 1999).

The introduction of compulsory teaching qualifications from September 2001

The government's post-compulsory education policy has been to make lifelong learning a major policy priority, giving education and training prime importance in the effort to raise economic output and to bring about a more just and inclusive society (DfEE 1998). The desire to improve education and training has led the government to focus on raising the quality of teaching (DfEE 2000). Even in opposition, Labour gave some attention to the question of ITE and staff development for FE teachers, recognising that decisions under incorporation had been left for the marketplace and institutions themselves.

While the government did not carry through its pre-election pledge

(Davis 1997) to include FE college teachers in the General Teaching Council (GTC) for schools, the Secretary of State did provide considerably more money for FE colleges in 1999, contingent on colleges widening participation, improving student retention and achievement and improving the quality of teaching and learning. The government affirmed the importance of initial teacher education and the professional development of FE staff and managers (Blackstone 1998), and decided to continue the DfEE's payment of fees for those undergoing initial teacher education for the FE college sector, in line with the same policy for primary and secondary PGCE courses. In 1998, the government once again reiterated its wish to ensure that all new FE college staff were teacher-qualified (DfEE 1998).

In a colloquium on developing a framework for FENTO qualifications in July 1999, a paper produced by the DfEE set the scene, stating that soon all new teachers would need teaching qualifications, based upon the FENTO standards. It suggested that an intermediate qualification needed to be developed for part-time teachers in FE colleges and recommended that teacher qualifications would need to be modular to allow such flexibility (DfEE 1999a). The questions for discussion set out in the paper included what the qualifications should be called; at what academic level they should be set; how the qualifications could be assessed and how FENTO should go about kite-marking qualifications.

At a FENTO conference on 10 February 2000, the Minister for Lifelong Learning renewed the government's pledge to 'offer effective teaching and training by appropriately qualified staff who have the opportunities for continuing training and development' (DfEE 2000a: 2). The new Learning and Skills Council would be expected to offer contracts to only those providers who were able to demonstrate that they have reached the appropriate standards set by the inspectorate, rewarding the best providers, setting targets for weaker providers and challenging 'coasting providers'.

The need for FE teacher qualifications to raise the standards of teaching and learning and not act as a deterrent for part-time teachers or for existing full-time and part-time teachers was addressed. It was suggested that experienced teachers who were not appropriately qualified might get exemption but that 'these operate on a case by case basis rather than offering blanket exemption for all teachers falling within a particular group' (DfEE 2000: 5).

Compulsory teaching qualifications came into effect from September 2001 under Statutory Instrument 2001, No. 1209. This introduced the following requirements for new FE teachers:

a All new unqualified teachers who become employed to teach an FE course leading to a nationally recognised qualification at an FE college will be required to hold, or work towards and achieve in a specified time, a recognised qualification appropriate to their role.

b Unqualified new full-time and fractional FE teachers will be required to gain a university Certificate in Education or equivalent within 2–4 years (two years for ft: longer for those on fractional contracts depending on hours worked).

c Unqualified new part-time teachers not on fractional contracts will be required to achieve a Stage 1 or Stage 2 Teaching Certificate – according to role (Stage 1 within one year, Stage 2 within two years).

FENTO standards: the endorsement process

Alongside the introduction of compulsory teacher education, university ITE programmes and awarding bodies such as City and Guilds were also required to submit their documentation to FENTO for approval or endorsement from September 2001. FENTO stated that institutions mapping the standards against existing courses would be given endorsement for one year only, after which the institution must re-apply for endorsement (FENTO 2002).

In response to the endorsement requirement, some universities 'mapped' the standards to existing units of competence and modules in their Certificate of Education courses. Other universities adopted the FENTO standards and designed their courses accordingly, employing a student-focused, 'tick-box' approach in which individual student competencies are matched against the standards, as is the case for NVQs. Some other universities have used the standards as a means of judging the quality of the whole to the course – much as they would with FEFC college inspection criteria (UCET 2000).

In mapping the standards against existing courses, the question of applying educational or academic levels to the standards caused (and is still causing) considerable consternation (FEDA 1999a). For example, Wolverhampton University reported in 1998 that

> the standards do not give scope for indicating the quality or level of achievement. We would not expect inexperienced teachers to demonstrate their knowledge and skill in relation to a particular standard at the same level to that of experienced teachers.
>
> (University of Wolverhampton 1998: 4)

Some universities mapped their existing Certificate of Education and PGCE courses to the FENTO standards regardless of the academic level, be it level 3 (HE) or 'M' (masters) level. It seems possible therefore to 'cover' the FENTO standards in varying degrees of depth. One of the most important issues on the implementation side of the FENTO standards is their disaggregation in terms of academic levels. For example, the difference in standards appropriate to someone entering the profession in comparison to experienced teachers (DfEE 2000).

The irony was that colleges and universities were grappling with the opposite problem to the NVQ approach, which specified competencies in endless detail and became an increasingly bureaucratic exercise for colleges, thereby making the assessment less accessible to the individual students it was supposed to empower (Wolf 1995). In the case of the FENTO standards, it was the very generality of the standards, welcomed by awarding bodies, which caused most consternation when applied in practice against existing courses (UCET 1999). This was because the FENTO standards were initially designed as a basis for an NVQ and not as generic TTA-type standards. In that respect, they remained occupational not professional standards. Even in 2003 researchers found confusion in universities regarding the level 'fourness' of standards and many universities were using the standards quite differently (Lucas *et al.* 2004).

The application of the standards in relation to levels and the three stages of FE ITE qualifications was, and is, unclear. In addition the 'mapping' of the standards against existing PGCE and Certificate of Education courses has been a mechanical and inconsistent exercise in which providers have complied with the endorsement exercise in terms of their documentation but little has actually changed in the content and delivery of ITE courses. This is illustrated by the Ofsted survey inspection (Ofsted 2003), which showed that despite the endorsement of ITE qualifications by FENTO a great deal of variety and uneven practice remained in terms of content, course hours and teaching practice visits in ITE provision across different universities and colleges (UCET 2003).

Alongside problems concerning the application of the FENTO standards, there are other issues that arise, such as the application of FENTO standards to the diverse practices of FE college teachers. There is little disagreement about the FENTO standards as such, although like all occupational standards or competencies, they are open to wide interpretation (Elliott 2000). Mahony and Hextall (2000), in a study of standards applied to the school sector distinguished between two contrasting orientations to standards. The first is the 'developmental orientation', which views standards as a means of providing structured opportunities for teachers to develop and improve the quality of what they do. The second orientation is a 'regulatory orientation', which uses the standards as a tool to improve the efficiency of an individual teacher's performance by standardising practice. Applying these distinctions to the FENTO standards suggests that the main emphasis given to the implementation of FENTO standards and the endorsement process has been overwhelmingly 'regulatory', in the sense that its major emphasis has been to standardise ITE programmes. In that respect there may be a useful distinction to be drawn between occupational (regulatory) and professional (developmental) standards.

Some regulation is clearly necessary to bring a greater coherence to ITE and staff development programmes. When the endorsement process started FENTO emphasised that the process of endorsement aimed to develop teaching qualifications and not simply to endorse existing qualifications.

In practice, however, such laudable aims were limited by resources and circumstances and the endorsement process to date has been rather regulatory in the sense that it has led to a narrow focus on the 'coverage' or 'mapping' of the standards against existing courses. In other words, FENTO found itself stuck with a set of occupational standards that were not designed for developmental purposes.

During the endorsement process, documentation was scrutinised but the process was essentially a paper-based exercise which did not view lessons or ask the opinions of learners. The danger here is that this 'coverage' or 'mapping' does not taken account of the wider context in which professional practice takes place in the FE college sector (Bathmaker 1999). As a consequence, the application of FENTO standards is being treated as a technical issue that belittles the status of knowledge and understanding (Hyland and Merrill 2003). Such a mechanical application of standards does not recognise the historical diversity and differences in the practices of FE teachers, or that many candidates on ITE courses in universities and colleges are work-based educators/trainers, outside the DfES definition of the FE college sector yet included by the Learning and Skills Council within further education. Furthermore, the mechanical mapping of FENTO standards takes no account of the need to develop new professional practices in the light of the growing diversity of student needs.

Overall, the implementation of the FENTO standards is taking place within the context of an impoverished professional culture that has a tendency towards compliance. As a consequence the standards are being implemented in a mechanical way, focusing on how students can 'generate evidence against the standards' (Fawbett 2003). In such a scenario there seems to be no recognition of the difficult balance to be struck between the regulation of existing programmes and the need to improve the quality of professional practice across a wide variety of courses that reflect very different cultures and professional practices.

There has been no independent research carried out on the endorsement process. FENTO itself has carried out its own evaluation; 70 per cent of providers who responded said the endorsement process had added value to their qualification (FENTO 2002). Such claims do not reflect evidence of growing dissatisfaction with the FENTO endorsement process, the criticisms of the standards raised by Ofsted (2003), and the fact that many ITE providers are wondering what the role, function and powers of FENTO are when Ofsted is taking responsibility for inspecting ITE qualifications (UCET 2003a). In any case, awarding bodies will not be openly critical of a regulatory body that is endorsing their ITE qualifications (providers tend to tell regulatory bodies what they think they want to hear). Perhaps because of this the FENTO findings have little validity. Rather unsurprisingly, early evidence suggests a very uneven application of the endorsement process, depending on the views and past experience of the endorsement reviewers (UCET 2003a).

While the endorsement process has not had a positive influence on standards of teaching in FE, it has further highlighted the unevenness of teaching practice hours and teacher-led input hours on ITE qualifications. The fear is that, in the absence of a professional culture that has agreed practices or discusses teaching and learning, the mechanical mapping-type process of FENTO endorsement could lead to a greater standardisation of practice. This may be regarded as good in some respects, yet in other ways it weakens one of the important strengths of FE; the diversity of practice to meet the diversity of learner needs and learning contexts.

Conclusion

The introduction of compulsory teacher qualifications and the idea of national standards have been welcomed by most universities and FE colleges, many of which acknowledge that there was hitherto an unacceptable variation in the structure and quality of ITE and professional development arrangements. However, the FENTO national standards were arrived at through functional mapping, initially designed to be the basis of an NVQ. After consultation FENTO did abandon the NVQ model, but was left with occupational standards designed for a different purpose. While few disagree with the FENTO standards as such, they remain occupational standards for an NVQ and are of very little actual use in improving the quality of ITE programmes. As such they remain a sort of 'hybrid' that falls between providing a professional or 'industrial' framework for FE teachers.

Because of the origins of the standards the endorsement process carried out by FENTO became a procedure where ITE courses had to prove that they 'covered' the occupational standards as they would competences. As a result awarding bodies, colleges and many universities mechanically 'mapped' the standards against their existing diverse ITE provision and focused on 'covering' the standards however superficially. Such an approach did not take into account the diverse contexts in which FE teachers practice and as a consequence the whole endorsement process became something of a mechanical affair that treated FE teachers as technicians.

Overall and throughout the period under discussion there has been some advance towards a more strategic and professional approach to ITE and professional development. FENTO standards have taken FE teachers some way towards a professional framework as, in the end, they represented FE teachers' rejection of an NVQ-type professional qualification. In that sense, the standards can be seen as an advance. Yet at the same time they remain a barrier because as occupational standards they cannot deliver a professional framework to raise the quality of teaching in further education. The next chapter discusses the impending demise of FENTO and the choices facing FE teachers – namely to become part of an employer-led Sector Skills Council and remain within the competence employer-led framework, or to seek a new professional framework along the lines of schoolteachers.

Notes

1 For example, the City and Guilds package individual TDLB units into 'mini-vocational qualifications': D32 and D33 for assessors; D34 and D35 for internal verifiers and D36 for APL Advisors.
2 The MCI was a lead body that established Occupational Standards for managers developed by the National Forum for Management Education.
3 See chapter 5.
4 This information is based on a note/minutes from an FEU seminar that took

place on 14 October 1994. A phone call to NCVQ was made at the meeting to inquire about the possibility of the NCVQ kitemarking university ITE programmes. The reply from the NCVQ was that this issue was not yet resolved. The NCVQ dealt with national organisations and would find it difficult dealing with a large number of separate universities. It was agreed to have a meeting with the NCVQ to see if the NCVQ's criteria and terms of reference could be changed so they could become more like the CNAA where course documentation had to be approved by the council.

5 The UPDC was set up to verify NVQ awards level 4 and 5 in order to prevent the NCVQ from doing so (Cantor *et al.* 1995).

6 Although observers were invited from the Scottish and Northern Ireland Offices, the development of the standards only involved consultation in Wales and England. Neither Scotland nor Northern Ireland were consulted even though they are part of the NTO structure.

7 It also drew on the work of the TDLB, MCI, TTA, SENTEC/SKILL, as well as UCET's work on standards for initial teacher training for FE.

8 Which only included England and Wales.

9 As discussed in chapter 3, NTOs were to rationalise the Industry Lead Bodies, yet in the information sent out about NTOs by the DfEE (1998a) a column indicating which NTOs replaced former LIBs or ITOs, showed that 36 out of 39 NTOs were replacing only one other former lead industry body.

10 SPRITO for example, the NTO for the sports and recreation sector, was involved in a project to improve GNVQs by making them more relevant to employers. It was working on a project in partnership with schools and colleges to develop good practice and initiate optional units linked to NVQ competencies. This was funded by FEDA and recommendations were to go to the Qualifications and Curriculum Authority (QCA) (NTONC 1999a).

11 Called PAULO, after Paulo Freire.

7 The future shape of teacher education: professionalism or obscurity?

The end of FENTO: enter the Sector Skills Council?

On the premise that National Training Organisations (NTOs) had replicated the earlier Lead Industry Bodies, the Secretary of State for Education and Skills, announced in October 2001 the setting up of Sector Skills Councils (SSCs). These new employer-led bodies covered larger areas of the economy and replaced NTOs from April 2002 (Morris 2001). Consequently, although FENTO only started the endorsement process in September 2001, it officially ceased to exist from April 2002. However, despite its official demise, at the time of writing FENTO continues with the endorsement process, runs an FE teachers' help-line, continues to endorse awarding bodies offering ITE programmes, undertakes a number of research and development projects, is introducing minimum levels in Maths and English for all FE college teachers, and is overseeing the introduction of subject specifications in numeracy, literacy and ESOL. Most of these activities are funded by the DfES on a short-term basis. The legal status of FENTO as a regulatory body in such circumstances is far from clear, and the future of FENTO can only be seen in the short term.

At the time of writing, no SSC has yet been approved that includes the FE college sector. In 2002 FENTO tried to initiate progress towards a post-16 SSC against the background of an absence of strategic leadership being given by government bodies or departments. In September 2002, FENTO reported that negotiations were taking place with the Higher Education Staff Development Agency (HESDA) concerning the formation of a post-16 SSC (FENTO 2002).[1] However, the NTO covering adult and community education (PAULO) was, at that time, not involved in the negotiation and was busy trying to set up an Informal Learning SSC.

Both proposals went to the Sector Skills Development Agency (SSDA) and were rejected on the grounds of being too narrow to make a sufficient strategic and economic impact.

In 2003, a new initiative was taken to form a Lifelong Learning Sector Skills Council (LLLSSC), this time with the help of the DfES. The new LLLSSC was to build on the achievements of the former NTOs and take strategic control of workforce planning and development for the lifelong learning sector and 'meet the workforce need of employers in all other sectors' (Mackey 2003). The lifelong learning sector was to made up of community-based learning and development, employment- and work-based learning, further education, higher education, libraries, distributed learning and information services. All of these had formerly been NTOs and had functioning boards.

Despite unresolved tensions, a proposal for a shadow board has been developed, with FENTO receiving five of the 17 seats on the board. It is not at all clear how smaller NTOs will get a hearing or what the function of the LLLSSC will be in relation to Ofsted (which now inspects all teacher training qualifications for the post-compulsory sector), the new DfES Standards Unit and the Learning and Skills Councils. The uncertainty about the role of the LLLSSC is compounded by a DfES document outlining its vision for the future of further education in which neither FENTO nor a new LLLSSC is mentioned at all, except that SSCs 'are significant employer bodies, licensed by Government, that will lead the drive to significantly improve productivity in industry and business sectors throughout the UK' (DfES 2002a: 23).

Much still remains to be clarified concerning the role of this new sector skills council. The DfES sees its role ranging from being a strategic workforce planning body to being an organisation 'that harmonises LLL standards across all business sectors' (Mackey 2003). Furthermore, like NTOs, the new Sector Skills Councils need to be UK-wide, spanning, in the case of FE colleges, quite different traditions and standards in FE colleges in Scotland and Northern Ireland. One of the difficulties of establishing a Sector Skills Council is that it requires approval of, or may be vetoed by, any of the four nations that make up the UK. Such agreement is difficult to achieve as each nation is developing its own educational agenda and there is little support for FENTO in Scotland (FENTO 2002), yet it is hoped to submit an expression of interest and secure approval by June 2004.

It would seem that there are tensions and conflicts of interest in the merger of the former NTOs; no part wants to be 'swamped' by the others. In this respect, FENTO is by far the most influential NTO in its patch (Hoare and Kingston 2003) and in that sense has most to lose. How such matters as the endorsement of FE teacher qualifications and the introduction of a form of qualified teacher status will be brought about remains unclear. One suggestion is for the endorsement process to be carried out by a LLSSC 'trading company'.

Tom Bewick, who was a part of the government policy team that set up Sector Skills Councils, has argued that SSCs will 'shape training in each industrial sector' and the key to the success of SSCs is to get influential employers behind the drive to raise skills. He states that 'despite the rhetoric of business leadership, the network has yet to attract one household name or senior captain of industry'; the way to achieve this would be to provide leadership away from the people who previously ran second-rate NTOs, whose mindset was to 'screw as much public cash as possible out of the treasury' (Bewick 2003: 4).

Importantly, attempts to form an employer-led Sector Skills Council for FE college teachers are somewhat less than appropriate. If schoolteachers, university lecturers and other professionals have no such organisations, why is it that teachers in FE colleges and the wider learning and skills sector need an employer-led body to set standards and verify qualifications? As Huddleston and Unwin (2002) suggest, FE colleges are now part of an employer-led learning and skills sector with leading figures from the 'business community' in control of National and Local Learning and Skills Councils as well as Sector Skills Councils. The government appears to be placing the same faith in the 'business community' that characterised education and training from the late 1970s, a period that has not been judged a success. This is to say nothing of the fact that the new bodies mentioned above are replacing the employer-led

Technical Education Councils (TECs) that were also judged to be a failure (Huddleston and Unwin 2002). There is little evidence of employer-led bodies succeeding. In fact there is a lot of evidence to the contrary. Raggatt and Williams (1999) show that so-called employer-led bodies in the 1980s and 1990s that set up the NVQ qualifications were not employer-led but dominated by officials. The authors suggest that the employers were not able to dedicate time to such bodies and that this is generally the fate of employer-led bodies. If it is the case that officials replace employers in these bodies, is it not fair to ask to whom the officials are accountable? And how are decisions made?

The DfES Standards Unit and the proposals for initial teacher education and professional development

Success for All: Reforming further education and training (DfES 2002b) made a number of important proposals on funding, widening participation, improving choice, regional planning and restructuring the sector. However, a large part of the document concerns teaching quality and teacher development, 'identify and disseminate good practice, learning materials and training programmes' (DfES 2002b: 12). Furthermore, the Standards Unit in the DfES will also identify teaching and learning methods and develop new teaching and learning frameworks (see table 7.1).[2]

Guidance for these frameworks will be provided by practitioners, who will in turn revise ITE programmes.[3] For each framework 'key deliverables' will include 'guidance to practitioners in a range of formats and media; an intensive face to face training programme delivered by practitioners to practitioners; revised initial teacher or trainer training; an ongoing support programme for practitioners and teaching and training materials including e-learning' (DfES 2002b: 31).

Targets are also set for teaching qualifications among FE college teachers (see table 7.2). By 2010, all existing FE teachers should be teacher-trained and new full-time entrants would need to be qualified within two years. All new part-time staff should be qualified within four years. An interim target has been set for 90 per cent of full-time and 60 per cent of

Table 7.1 *Learning frameworks*

Target dates	Subject areas to be covered
2003/4	Construction, Entry to Employment, Business Studies, Science
2004/5	Health and Social Care, Information and Computer Technology, Maths, Land Based FE (agriculture)
2005/6	seven other unspecified areas

part-time FE teachers to be qualified to teach or enrolled on appropriate courses by 2005/6. In order to reach these targets, the DfES is to 'transfer an element of the former standards fund into core funding for FE and sixth form colleges and plan to require colleges to set out their three year Development Plans – and then deliver – targets and approaches to developing the skills and qualifications of the staff' (DfES 2002b: 37).

Table 7.2 *Targets for teacher training*[4]

2005/6	90% Full-time teachers to be teacher-trained 60% Part-time teachers to be teacher-trained (Percentage calculated on those qualified or enrolled on appropriate courses)
2010	All existing teaching staff to be teacher-trained (New entrants must gain a teaching qualification within 2–4 years of appointment)

Success for All states that all initial teacher education courses will require approval by the Secretary of State. However, it says nothing concerning FENTO or a Lifelong Learning Sector Skills Council, although it does propose the development of an employer-led Sector Skills Council for the learning and skills sector to assess workforce development. It rather seems that the emphasis given to Sector Skills Councils varies according to which part of the DfES is writing documents and developing policy.[5]

The implications of requiring specialist qualifications for teachers of adult literacy, numeracy and ESOL

Following the Moser Report (1999), it was announced that all new teachers employed to teach literacy, numeracy and ESOL in FE colleges will be required to hold, or work towards and achieve in a specified time a specialist literacy, numeracy and ESOL teaching qualification (DfES 2002a). This meant that teachers of numeracy, literacy and ESOL, in addition to being part of the statutory framework and targets that apply to all FE teachers (discussed in chapter 6), were also required to obtain a subject specialist qualification at level 4 of the national qualification framework. These new specialist qualifications are required in addition to a general teaching qualification and are underpinned by the subject specifications developed and introduced by FENTO and the DfES Adult Basic Skills Strategy Unit (ABSSU). They define the knowledge, personal skills and understanding required of teachers of adult literacy, numeracy and ESOL. The subject specifications are designed to ensure that all new teachers of literacy, numeracy and ESOL are equipped with the appropriate and relevant knowledge, understanding and personal skills in their subject in order to put them on a par with teachers in any other subject area (DfES/FENTO 2002).

The decision to incorporate both pedagogic standards and subject specifications within the teacher education curriculum makes such programmes radically different from existing post-16 PGCEs and in-service Certificates of Education. Traditionally, post-16 ITE programmes assumed that trainee teachers already had adequate subject knowledge; they therefore concentrated on pedagogic issues. The new courses are required to deliver both subject and pedagogic knowledge with the expressed view of improving the quality of teaching.

Several new courses piloted in 2002/3 were included in a National Research and Development Centre (NRDC) research and evaluation project (Lucas *et al.* 2004). The researchers found that the problem faced by the course developers was how to bring subject knowledge and practical teaching knowledge together. It is important here to distinguish between learning to teach through a focus on a trainee's subject or vocational knowledge and the teaching of the subject knowledge itself that under-pins all teaching. In other words, the key issue is how different types of knowledge are re-contextualised (Bernstein 2000), or relating one type of knowledge to the other in ways that enhance practice. This is a funda-mental pedagogic problem that all teacher educators face. However, this is particularly acute in ITE programmes that incorporate the teaching of subject knowledge. Here the goal is not just to teach a subject for its own sake (as in academic undergraduate or MA programmes) but to enhance the quality of teaching in these subject areas.[6] In other words, the pro-grammes present a new challenge of relating 'what you teach' and 'how you teach it', along with a deeper understanding of the subject area.

Like the Ofsted report discussed below, the NRDC report also identified a diverse range of trainees with significant differences in terms of pur-poses, needs and expectations. The report argued that this has important implications for providers in relation to how the training programmes are structured, how theoretical and practical aspects of training are inte-grated, and how differentiation and optional elements are built into the programmes. Tutors and trainees had different views about the sequenc-ing of elements of the programmes and the different needs of sub-groups within the cohorts. It was evident, for example, that 'novices' needed some initial input of subject knowledge before they could be expected to begin to develop pedagogic skills. In such a case a strategic decision can be taken to sequence theory (subject knowledge) before practice (practical pedagogy) in the course structure. Course designers of other programmes took other strategic decisions such as integrating subject knowledge and practical pedagogy, which illustrates possible sequencing options for course designers in order that knowledge can be organised to meet the individual needs of trainees. The different emphasis and content given to novices and experienced practitioners has also been discussed in research on generic ITE courses (Harkin *et al.* 2003). This issue high-lights the incompatibilities of providing the same course to meet the enormous diversity of the cohorts taking the level 4 ITE qualifications.

Interestingly, the research also highlighted two different approaches that providers seemed to be adopting towards the subject specifications (which may also be applied to the FENTO standards). The first approach the report called the 'knowledge based approach'. This reflects the academic tradition of subject knowledge based on a 'need to know' basis. This approach is similar to the way in which a syllabus is interpreted in most academic subjects. The teacher selects which bits to emphasise and how much depth is given to each particular bit, according to their interpretation of what the student needs to know to be able pass the final examination. The report suggested that some teachers took this approach because it was how they had always approached a syllabus, while others used it as a means of coping with the difficulties of teaching the subject specifications in terms of time, level, depth and breadth.

The second approach the researchers called the 'standards based approach' and this reflected the vocational tradition of the 'need to do'. This approach emphasised 'coverage' or 'mapping' the course against each standard or specification in order that everything is covered. It works from the assumption that knowledge is implicit in performance. Such an approach is associated with the competence tradition of national vocational qualifications and emphasises 'coverage', as in the FENTO endorsement process.

These two approaches to the subject specification (which can also be applied to the FENTO standards) do not fit easily together and reflect wider debates concerning how best to organise professional education and training and what emphasis to give to theory and practice and how the two are related.

The report raises many important issues outside of the focus on subject specifications including the fundamental pedagogic problem that all teacher educators face – namely that of relating theory and practice and finding ways of linking both subject teaching and learning theory to practice and the sequence in which they take place in the programme. What makes these new programmes particularly challenging is that they include all the old problems of teacher education with the added problem of including the teaching of subject knowledge to a very diverse group of trainees.

The introduction of core subject knowledge for all teacher education programmes

The debate about introducing minimum qualifications in areas such as maths and English has been going on for some time. As illustrated in chapter 6, this was the subject of much debate with the introduction of compulsory ITE qualifications in FE and again when subject specifications were developed for basic skills teachers, as discussed above. While all sides agreed that some minimum requirement in core skills should be a requirement for all FE college teachers, there were differences about what level it should be, the form it should take and how it was to be assessed. A particular concern was expressed concerning teachers in vocational areas who may find such requirements daunting.

Without consultation with ITE providers, FENTO announced in August 2003 that from September 2003 all generic teacher education programmes should begin the process of including a level 3 core in language, literacy and numeracy. These specifications were based upon the existing level 3 subject specification in these three areas required by teaching assistants.[7] Providers were encouraged to audit their programmes in 2003/4 to investigate ways of including the outstanding elements in suitable areas of their programmes. It was announced that this must be fully implemented by September 2004 and be checked by FENTO at the same time as the general standards for teaching and supporting learning.

In the weeks that followed the letter from FENTO, ITE providers did not argue against the idea of a minimum level in the areas of language, literacy and numeracy – that was common ground. The focus of objection was the lack of consultation and the consequent doubts that the initiative had been thought through carefully. For example, providers asked why FE teachers needed level 3 when school teachers were only required to demonstrate level 2 knowledge to get their QTS, and why ICT was excluded when it was part of the skills test for school teachers.

No extra resources were offered to providers to meet the new requirement – although the review of funding discussed below had not yet been published. No guidance was given on the assessment of the specifications and it seemed that providers were to 'integrate' the level 3 subject specifications into existing programmes following a process of mapping subject specifications against existing provision. Nothing was said regarding the particular concern that teachers from vocational backgrounds might find level 3 in English and maths too much of a jump. Providers wanted the opportunity to discuss a more flexible means of meeting the core knowledge, suggesting that providers should adopt a different approach to trainees who have degrees or equivalent and those entering from vocational fields where little prior certificated qualifications have traditionally been required.[8]

The introduction of minimum standards for all FE college teachers in language, literacy and numeracy is something that most ITE providers see as necessary. One is left wondering, however, why policy makers did not use and amend the existing TTA level 2 tests, at least for a trial period.[9] The TTA QTS skills tests have a track record, have been tried and tested, are provided on a website and have flexible means of support (TTA 2003). They were established at considerable expense, with the TTA computerised tests being taken in training centres. Candidates must pass these tests to gain QTS status, but no limit is put on attempts to pass. Furthermore, the TTA numeracy, literacy and ICT skills tests are set in the context of the wider professional role of the teacher. In other words, the knowledge tested is applied to the kinds of requirements faced by teachers in their day-to-day work. For example, the numeracy test starts with audio mental arithmetic tests; the literacy test starts with spelling, punctuation, and grammar; the ICT tests start with word processing, presentation packages, databases and spreadsheets, and so on.

Another area of confusion concerns whether language, literacy and numeracy are to be specifically and separately assessed. The experience of key skills in GNVQs would suggest that if key skills are not assessed separately they become 'integrated out'. This 'embedded approach' to key skills in GNVQs was criticised in the mid-1990s by the school inspectorate because it did not allow for the systematic development of mathematical and language skills (Spours 1997). There is the danger that if these key areas are not assessed separately they will not be taken seriously by trainers or trainees and the whole exercise will mirror the

'FENTO fandango' (Lucas 2004), where complying becomes a paper-based, technical, mapping game with little actually changing in the delivery of courses.

The reform of FE teacher education: the Ofsted survey report and DfES response

While debate continued over minimum key skills for FE teachers, the first Ofsted national survey report was published in November 2003.[10] The report focused on the system of FE teacher education and its ability to meet the needs of trainees and was based upon visits to eight higher education institutions and 23 FE colleges. It concluded: 'the current system of FE teacher training does not provide a satisfactory foundation of professional development for FE teachers at the start of their careers' (Ofsted 2003: 4).

The report maintained that while the taught elements of the course were generally good, other elements were weak. These included critical areas such as practical teaching, mentoring in the workplace and gaining a broad experience of education and training. The report pointed out that the main weakness in the current system arises from defects in these wider aspects of teacher education. The most striking aspect focused on the lack of subject-specific knowledge and pedagogy given to trainees, which it considered to be the major weakness displayed by many trainees. This included a limited knowledge of the teaching methods necessary to develop subject-specific or occupation-specific knowledge and skills because 'the mainly generic training they receive does not equip them for teaching highly specialised subjects or groups of students with special needs' (Ofsted 2003: 32–3).

The report focused on three major areas. The first of these was meeting the individual learning needs of trainees. Although the taught elements of ITE courses in HEIs and colleges were considered generally good in the sense of being well planned and delivered, Ofsted found the training programmes were insufficiently differentiated to meet the extremely wide ability range and experience of trainees. As a consequence, some trainees struggled with the demands of work at HE level, while others found the programmes undemanding. Ofsted established that important basic information and qualifications of trainees were not known and the individual needs of the diverse group of trainees were not adequately assessed at the start of the courses. The survey recorded that about half of trainees lacked level 2 qualifications in literacy and about two-thirds lacked level 2 qualifications in numeracy; little was done to meet the learning needs of the trainees in these key areas. Furthermore, while the tuition that trainees received on the taught elements of their courses was generally good, too few opportunities were provided for trainees to learn how to teach their specialist subjects, and there were too few connections made between the taught elements of the course and the supervision and assessment of trainees' practical teaching.

Second, the report focused on the lack of consistent support given to trainees in the colleges while they were undertaking practical teaching sessions. The survey report found a lack of systematic mentoring in the workplace, with the trainees' progress being inhibited by insufficient observation and feedback on their teaching. As a consequence of this, little use was being made of individual action plans and setting clear learning goals. The report suggested that the observation of teaching does not have a high enough profile in assessment, observations were rarely carried out by a subject specialist, and the procedures for teaching observation were generally no guarantee that someone awarded a teaching qualification was a competent classroom or workshop teacher. The lack of systematic and effective subject-specialist mentoring arrangements for trainees was considered a major systemic weakness. Ofsted found that in the few places where mentoring arrangements did exist they led to the development of good teaching skills in their subject. The question of ensuring the provision of workplace mentoring to support trainees to develop subject-specialist teaching skills was given the highest priority in the recommendations of the report

Third, Ofsted evaluated the effectiveness of the FENTO standards. It reported that while the standards provide a useful outline of the capabilities required of experienced FE teachers, they do not clearly define the standards required of new teachers. As a consequence, FENTO standards are of limited value in securing common understanding of the pass/fail borderline on courses of initial training or judging the attainment of newly qualified teachers. Furthermore, the survey found that most trainees said the language of the standards was remote and they seldom used the standards to increase their knowledge and skill because there were far too many standards and subheadings. Ofsted reported that the standards themselves do not take insufficient account of the differing experiences and contexts of teaching in FE, do not cover the demands made by 14–16-year-olds, and give insufficient attention to subject or occupational pedagogy. What is more, the FENTO standards were said to be an inappropriate tool for designing ITT courses and inappropriate for the wider learning and skills sector that needed separate standards.

The Ofsted report made the following recommendations.

HEIs and national awarding bodies should:
• give substantially more attention to developing trainees' expertise in teaching their subject;
• ensure that the trainees' practical teaching is made more central to their training and assessment;
• take more account of the diverse needs of trainees in designing training programmes.

FE colleges should:
• integrate ITT with their overall management of human resources, including the professional development of staff;
• ensure the provision of workplace mentoring to support trainees in developing the necessary skills to teach their specialist subjects.

The Department for Education and Skills (DfES) should:
• work with FENTO to identify those of the current standards which are most appropriate to the initial training of FE teachers;
• consider how to link the current standards for school teachers with those for FE teachers and other trainers working in the learning and skills sector;
• review the adequacy of funding arrangements for FE teacher training to support the changes indicated above.

                                                                    (Ofsted 2003: 4–5)

As Ofsted launched its survey report at the AoC conference in late 2003 the DfES simultaneously launched its response in the form of a consultation paper, entitled *The Future of Initial Teacher Education for the Learning and Skills Sector: An agenda for reform* (DfES 2003).

Importantly, the emphasis of the DfES report was quite different from that of Ofsted. For a start, its brief encompassed the whole learning and skills sector, not just teachers in FE colleges. Furthermore, in contrast to Ofsted's comments on the inadequacy of the FENTO standards and process, the DfES consultation document stated that 'the quality of FE initial teacher education courses is assured by FENTO through their process of endorsement' (DfES 2003: 7). It mentioned NVQs in learning and development and the employment national training organisation standards for learning and development, and in its opening page, placed FENTO standards within an NVQ framework.

Throughout the DfES report, the emphasis differed from that of Ofsted, reflecting a different approach to the regulation of FE teacher education programmes. Ofsted looked towards the schoolteacher model as a way forward. The DfES recommended a strengthened FENTO endorsement type process that would become the responsibility of the as yet unformed LLLSSC.[11] The endorsement process of the LLLSSC would include a check on initial assessment of trainees, their individual learning plans and professional development record, and a formalised mentoring process. It would also ensure that moderation procedures for teaching practice visits and assessment take place, and that the endorsement process should include a check on the suitability of the teacher educators in such areas as recent and relevant experience and appropriate qualifications.

The DfES consultation document proposed an entitlement for all trainee teachers and an opportunity for all those who are suitably qualified to gain the status of Qualified Teacher of Further Education (DfES 2003: 4). The entitlement also includes a professional formation stage which encompasses initial training and 'workplace development'; an initial assessment, leading to differentiated learning according to individual need; observation of trainees' teaching and constructive feedback at appropriate intervals; mentoring support and a reduced teaching load during 'workforce development'.

The DfES review of funding for ITT in the post-16 sector

Quite separate to the Ofsted and DfES reports discussed above, the question of the level of funding for FE ITE programmes has become an increasingly important issue. It has been difficult to calculate how much extra funding is required to deliver the subject specifications in literacy, numeracy and ESOL as well as the FENTO standards. During early 2003, an attempt was made within an NRDC research project (Lucas *et al.* 2004) to calculate the funding level of ITE FE programmes and the extra costs of delivering the subject specifications, but it was found difficult to do so. In the light of this lack of clarity, PricewaterhouseCoopers (PwC) was commissioned by the DfES Standards Unit to undertake an audit and a review of funding for initial teacher training for the post-16 sector (PwC 2003).

In setting the broader context for understanding funding, the report found surprisingly similar areas of concern highlighted in the Ofsted and NRDC reports mentioned above. For example, there was much variety of practice in ITE programmes, with teaching practice visits varying from two to 12 and teaching hours on courses showing a wide variation. Also found was a wide range of qualifications, delivery methods and modes with the level of teaching assessment varying widely across providers and courses. Commenting on FENTO, PwC said that HEIs had concerns about the FENTO standards, suggesting that they were not fit for purpose being 'too much like NVQ assessments'. PwC also concluded that there was a lack of clarity in the relationship between FENTO and providers and that what is required is 'a single body responsible for standard setting and inspection against those standards' (PwC 2003: para. 136).

PwC also uncovered significant variations in cost that did not necessarily reflect itself in staff–student contact time. They found that the current funding was complex and inconsistent, reflecting a limited understanding by providers of what should 'be delivered in the current cost envelope'. They found 'widely varying patterns of cost and income and therefore of surplus and deficit'. High costs tended to be driven by overhead regimes and massive 'top slicing' (varying from 0 to 64 per cent), by different pedagogical approaches or by accounting factors such as institutional approaches to payment for travel time.

The PwC report described the patterns of funding and costs as 'capricious'. Many providers had little idea about the actual income they received. For example, it was reported by providers that on part-time courses HEFCE funding varied from £500 to £1,900, LSC funding from £270 to £565 and fees from zero to £1,048. Of the 28 HEI courses examined, 13 enjoyed a surplus and 15 were in deficit.

After correcting their figures to take a number of 'anomalous factors' into consideration, such as anomalous sets of data for one course and excessive overhead charges from another, the report concluded that costs and income were in a 'broad balance', although if additional teaching was required in the future funding 'may cease to cover costs'.[12] The statement that the cost and income were in 'broad balance' was qualified in the report by introducing the idea of 'cost endogeneity'. This describes the natural tendency for public sector costs to be determined by the amount of funding rather than by the market. In this case, the finding of PwC that the funding is broadly equal to the costs does not imply that the level is right. Costs may have settled at a level too low or too high. The report suggest that 'everyone and no one' is responsible for FE ITT, and that a single-minded oversight from one agency is recommended, which should be 'the TTA or an agency operating in broadly the same way'.

Conclusion

In recent years there has been a plethora of reports and documents concerning the reform of initial teacher education for the further education teacher. This represents a big change from the 'benign neglect' of the past and there is much to be welcomed regarding the raising of standards of ITE programmes. In the forthcoming discussion regarding the future of FE ITE there are many detailed and strategic issues to be discussed and resolved. Here, the focus is on three main areas of concern.

The first is the new emphasis given to subject knowledge and giving subject-specific practical support to trainees in the workplace. Both of these issues are important. Nonetheless, in emphasising subject knowledge and improving subject support certain balances and contextual factors need to be taken into account. Clearly, improving a trainee's knowledge of their actual subject or vocational specialism would be a major advance and the current lack of it is a major systemic weakness in FE ITE programmes. It is through practical teaching that trainees have the opportunity to make sense of (recontextualise) what they have learned. Supported teaching with a mentor in the workplace is a crucial learning zone if trainees are to reach their full potential. However, to provide such support is easier said then done and there are dangers in focusing too narrowly on subject/vocational expertise. As chapters 4 and 9 illustrate, there is a strong tradition in FE of teachers seeing vocational or subject expertise as far more important than having a knowledge of teaching. FE colleges have different subject traditions and cultures, reflected in departments that are often linked into narrow conceptions of teaching and learning. FE teachers, too, have an impoverished professional culture that, as yet, has few common professional understandings or agreed standards of professional practice. In these circumstances, the subject support given to FE teachers needs to be balanced by wider professional influences in order to avoid limiting the trainees' understanding to their own subject/vocational area. It is important that pedagogies in other subjects are considered and wider aspects of students' learning understood.

Furthermore, there are real doubts that at present the expertise exists in some subject areas in colleges to provide mentor support to trainees. Where provision is small, only one teacher may be involved and giving subject support would require some form of regional subject network. Added to this there is also some anxiety that in some subject/vocational areas, the pool of expertise and experience needed for mentoring does not as yet exist. ESOL is a good example. Much more thinking needs to be done on providing mentor support with a strategic rethinking of partnerships between FE colleges and universities and perhaps in the short term a special fund to allow expert support to be brought in by the partnerships. The Ofsted draft framework for inspection (HMI 2004) contains within it a potential unintended consequence that universities will not provide ITE places for certain vocational and subject areas because of a lack of confidence that subject support can be provided in the workplace. For some universities it may be better to take only certain types of trainees and subject/vocational areas than be faced with a poor Ofsted report – after all HEIs have very little control over what support is provided to trainees in colleges. If on the other hand, HEIs only took those trainees where they had subject expertise it would not correspond to the diversity of FE. The irony is that the Ofsted survey report highlighted the problems of FE ITE as being systemic, yet its own consultation on an inspection framework takes little account of the wider systemic context.

The second area of concern is more strategic. It seems clear from all recent documents that the government is determined to set up Sector Skills Councils, which many agencies such as NATFHE and the AoC seem resigned to, even though privately they have grave reservations. However, such a direction may be inappropriate given that the whole SSC strategy is based upon an industrial and business model working to essentially occupational standards. Teachers in further education, like teachers in schools and higher education, should be firmly located in a professional model with professional, not occupational, standards.

The new Lifelong Learning SSC (LLLSSC) will, according to the DfES, take strategic control of workforce planning and development for the lifelong learning sector and 'meet the workforce need of employers in all other sectors' (Mackey 2003). Nothing is said here about the professional needs of FE teachers. No other profession has SSCs. School teachers and university lectures have the GTC and the ILT (soon to become the 'Academy'). Why is it, then, that teachers in FE are singled out to require an employer-led body to set professional standards and verify qualifications? Why should FE teacher qualifications alone be led by leading figures from the 'business community'?

Importantly, recent policies such as the introduction of national standards and compulsory teacher education have been nudging FE teachers towards a professional framework and away from the industrial NVQ type route. Furthermore, the recent Ofsted survey on teacher education for FE teachers (Ofsted 2003) made fundamental criticisms of existing FE teacher education, suggesting a fundamental shake up which could include minimum key qualifications, subject-focused initial training and professional development, planned work-based subject support and proper mentoring for teachers in colleges, a proper professional development framework, the introduction of a probationary period and a form of FE QTS. Is this really going to be done by a focusing on the workforce needs of all other industrial sectors by an ill-defined LLLSSC?

The Ofsted survey report also suggested that the DfES look to the school-based route to learn lessons, and the PwC report on funding suggested that the TTA or an agency operating in a similar way is recommended. Could it be possible that FE teacher education could have bodies similar to that of the Teacher Training Agency and have a professional body like the GTC that could give FE teachers a professional status? The choice is between a professional framework similar to that of schoolteachers with newly qualified teacher (NQT) status and a form of qualified teacher status (QTS) or an industrial, competence-based model in the skills sector.

The third area of concern is that of regulating the old FEFC sector within the wider learning and skills sector. Much of the debate concerning FENTO occupational standards has focused on the difficulty of applying any one set of standards to the diverse set of learners and learning contexts within FE. Is it credible or desirable that one set of standards can apply across such a wide range of provision and learning contexts, ranging from sixth-form college provision to workplace learning? Specifying in any sort of detail what teachers and trainers should be doing in all these diverse learning contexts is a forlorn project. In that sense the FENTO occupational standards should be abandoned and a new approach towards standards adopted. One alternative option is to put in place a framework of professional standards that could be a 'core', with different contexts setting their own standards or professional practice.

Furthermore, is it possible at present to put in place regulations that can apply across the entire learning and skills sector? At the moment only FE teachers are required to be teacher-qualified, to have minimum qualifications in key skills and to work to a set of national standards. Workplace teachers/trainers are not regulated or inspected in the same way. Can QTS, entitlements that go along with the idea of NQT and compulsory ITE and minimum 'key skills' be applied right across the diverse learning and skills sector?

Notes

1 Why an NTO for higher education (HE) is joining a post-16 Sector Skills Council when HE is excluded from the learning and skills sector and the control of the Learning and Skills Council remained a mystery.

2 The use of the words 'learning frameworks' refers to subject areas covered. Each framework will identify best practice in delivery methods, assessment methods, programme content and teaching and learning techniques.

3 How this revision of ITE courses will be co-ordinated with the FENTO endorsement process is not discussed.

4 See chapter 3 for a discussion on the three-year plans that colleges must submit to the LSC.

5 The London-based DfES seems only to pay lip service to the strategy yet the Mortfort based (ex Manpower Services Commission) gives the SSC far more prominence (see Raggatt and Williams 1999).

6 The only other ITE course that focuses on subject knowledge as well as teaching is the BEd for primary and secondary teachers.

7 The level 3 specifications were attached to the letter that was sent informing providers of this new requirement.

8 For example, in the areas of hairdressing or motor vehicle maintenance.

9 Perhaps with some amendment to give them a more post-16 context.

10 There had been a very brief HMI report on the training of teachers in further and adult education in 1991 (DES 1991).

11 Later in the consultation document a rather contradictory statement is made, that it is not yet determined whether endorsement will come under the LLLSSC remit. It has been suggested that the endorsement process could be contracted out to a private organisation.

12 The report acknowledges that none of the providers they visited thought the funding to be at all adequate.

Part 3

THE DIVERSITY OF TEACHING AND LEARNING IN FURTHER EDUCATION

8 Teaching and learning traditions in further education

Introduction

Part 3 stands back from the chronology of previous chapters to look at the bigger picture, offering a conceptual framework for making sense of the changing context in which FE teachers work. In moving beyond the analysis of historical and recent policy changes, this section identifies teaching and learning traditions, and models for understanding the professional practice of FE teachers. Finally, it puts forward proposals for restructuring the FE sector, for a new professional framework for FE teachers and for a way of rethinking the professional practice and knowledge base of FE teachers.

This chapter distinguishes eight teaching and learning traditions and considers their implications for the practice of FE teachers. The rationale is not to provide a comprehensive account of qualifications and curricula or to suggest that the diverse practices of FE teachers fit neatly into the identified categories. The aim is to create analytical categories that can be used to understand and illuminate the variety and diversity of approaches to teaching and learning and their implications for the practice of FE teachers.

Identifying teaching and learning traditions in FE

Until recently debate and research about teaching and learning in the FE sector has been very limited (FEFC 1999b) reflecting the traditional resistance of many FE managers and teachers to consider new ideas and approaches. The limited engagement of most FE teachers in discussions and research concerning teaching and learning has allowed the traditional methods of training, originally associated with apprenticeships, to continue to be the main method of delivering the vocational curriculum, which in turn has restricted discussion across the rest of the FE curriculum (Gleeson and Mardle 1980). This situation has meant that no coherent framework yet exists for FE practitioners to develop an understanding of the different strategies required to address the growing diversity of FE learners and the changing contexts in which FE teachers work.

There has been some discussion concerning the diverse curriculum programmes that are offered in FE, but this has mainly related to describing qualifications or to understanding constant policy change in these areas; not the diversity of approaches to teaching and learning that takes place in FE. A useful start in this respect may be achieved through a focus on the idea of 'teaching and learning traditions'. Distinguishing between teaching and learning traditions and discussing the different practices associated with them is at best an approximation. The difficulty of identifying and categorising professional practice is partly because of the diversity of the FE sector and partly because each tradition is changing under external pressures. Furthermore, many teachers in FE colleges teach on more than one type of programme (Avis *et al.* 2001), sometimes adopting more learner-centred and flexible approaches to teaching and learning.

Even where unambiguous categories can be identified, such as general education or NVQ and job-specific training, different and contested approaches to teaching and learning exist within each of them. For example, teaching and learning in engineering is different from that in art and design or hairdressing or nursery nursing courses (Reeves 1995), even though they are all located within the teaching and learning tradition of NVQs and job-specific training. It is also the case that there are contested pedagogic approaches within particular teaching and learning traditions. For example, in general education there is a lively debate between those categorised as either 'traditional' or 'progressive' (Bolton 1994), to say nothing of different approaches and ideas about teaching and learning that exist within subject specialisms and subject departments.

Some of the teaching and learning traditions that I discuss below are drawn from curriculum traditions in FE colleges identified by Huddleston and Unwin (1997). Other traditions reflect recent changes in the curriculum offered and changes in the delivery of teaching and learning in FE in order to meet the growing diversity of students. A number of newer approaches to teaching and learning are identified in response to new types of students that have entered FE colleges. These cut across curriculum traditions as well as some of the teaching and learning traditions that will be referred to.

General education

The general education tradition is primarily concerned with the teaching of a collection of separate branches of academic knowledge which 'have their own internal criteria of relevance and worth and which are deliberately detached from those of "everyday" life' (Edwards 1997: 15).[1] What constitutes the best teaching and learning is hotly contested, remains unclear and is subject to changing connotations and pressures (Mortimore 1999). Approaches to teaching general education have often been characterised as the difference between progressive and traditional education, in other words, between approaches to teaching that are learner-centred or didactic.

While some discussion has taken place in universities, the overwhelming bulk of the literature concerning the teaching and learning of general academic education has focused upon research conducted in schools on academic subjects (Pring 1985). Debates concerning the teaching and learning in general education have rarely included teachers in FE, although there has been some work concerning the differences between A-level teaching and GNVQs (Edwards *et al.* 1997). Nevertheless, despite the lack of focus on teaching and learning in FE colleges, much of the debate and culture has been carried over to FE as many teachers transfer from school teaching to FE teaching. It is also the case that some university initial teacher training courses for FE teachers have been influenced by research and ideas concerning teaching and learning from the school sector (Elliott 1998). The influences of these school-focused discussions about pedagogy have been mainly reflected in general education departments of FE colleges, where most A levels, access courses and GCSEs are placed.

General education represents the tradition of pedagogy which is predominantly didactic,[2] adopting a subject-focused (Bloomer 1997), teacher-centred approach. Although there are differences in A-level teaching and learning according to the subject being taught (Edwards *et al.* 1997), in general A-level teaching is still largely didactic (Macfarlane 1993), with teachers interpreting the syllabuses in abstract and theoretical ways leading to over-directed teaching (HMI 1991). Following the Curriculum 2000 reforms and the introduction of AS levels it has even been suggested that the introduction of AS exams after one year has led to an even more didactic approach by teachers (Hodgson and Spours 2003).

In further education colleges, the subject-focused approach to general education courses does not reflect the national curriculum, as in schools, but applies to the relatively new teaching of GCSEs and A levels in FE colleges.[3] Other courses, such as Higher National Diplomas and Certificates, float uneasily within this tradition because they include the teaching of some academic generalised knowledge, whilst also having a strong vocational bias reflecting some parts of the non-NVQ job-specific tradition and some parts of the tradition of general vocational qualifications such as BTEC National. A levels are primarily knowledge-based and, according to Bloomer, while practical work and experimentation is valued, these are placed in a 'subordinate relationship to theoretical knowledge' (Bloomer 1997: 60), with the teacher interpreting meaning (Meager 1997).[4] Teachers are supported by textbooks, specimen papers, reading lists and syllabuses:

> Students spend much of their time digesting their teacher's notes for use in writing practice essays for the final examination.... Good teachers may employ all sorts of extra stimuli to enthuse their students, but there is a widespread underlying uniformity.
>
> (Reeves 1995: 76)

Didactic teaching and the concept of 'knowledge transmission' can be important dimensions of teaching and learning when the aim is the effective delivery of content. However, this represents only a partial understanding of the actual process of learning (Young and Lucas 1999), whether it be knowledge, skills or culturally normative beliefs. Bloomer (1997) for example, argues that one of the fundamental weaknesses of didactic, subject-focused teaching is that it is based upon an epistemology that sees subjects as specific and separate from others.[5] Such an approach sees learning as an individual decontextualised process even though the boundaries between subjects are being increasingly challenged, and knowing and understanding are increasingly seen to require a grasp of the interconnections between things (Pring 1995).

NVQs and job-specific training

The tradition of training relates to two types of qualifications. First, the older training, and second, the newer, NVQ competence-based qualifications. Although many of the more traditional vocationally specific qualifications have now been subsumed within the NVQ qualifications framework, the majority of vocational qualifications still fall outside the NVQ framework (DfEE 1995a) and are offered in many colleges through awarding bodies such as the City and Guilds of London Institute, the Royal Society of Arts (RSA) Examination Board and Pitman Training.

Traditional training is associated with craft, technician and day-release students and has its roots in the Mechanics' Institutes of the nineteenth century and the establishment of technical colleges after the Second World War (see chapter 1). This training tradition is usually associated with preparing people for performing specified tasks, most often set in a work-based context (Ecclestone 1997), with little emphasis given to broader knowledge or underlying rationale. The main task for students is to copy 'good practice'. In this context there is little need for teachers or trainers to think about teaching styles and methods, or other pedagogic considerations (Venables 1967). According to Gleeson and Mardle (1980), the tradition of training considers expertise in a specific job as an adequate basis for transmitting job-specific skills in a didactic way in a classroom, or, following a more apprentice/master model, in a workshop. In common with general education, this tradition is also based upon the transmission principle of content (albeit a different content) but also the transmission of cultural/industrial norms.

Training programmes in the older training tradition aim to prepare people for employment, which leads Pring (1995) to describe this as 'the vocational tradition'. Specific knowledge and skill transmission is combined with a socialisation process that ensures acceptable behaviour in the particular occupational sector (Avis *et al.* 2001). Sometimes this preparation takes place through instruction in the workplace itself and sometimes this environment is simulated in the FE classroom or workshop (Reeves 1995). Training and instruction become the transmission of context-specific skills, where knowledge and understanding are secondary to performance (Mansfield 1990).

The establishment of the NVQ framework came about in the late 1980s because of a general belief that the methods of assessment used in vocational education were unclear (Wolf 1995), and that many qualifications did not meet the needs of the workplace. Furthermore, it was the belief of the government of the time that employers needed to be put more formally at the forefront of setting standards in terms of outcomes and competencies (Debling 1989).

What distinguished NVQs from earlier approaches to vocational training was less the use of employers for setting standards than the explicit defining of occupationally specific competencies (Hyland 1994).[6] According to Ecclestone 'NVQs were originally intended to take place in employment, with achievement of competence separated from the need to attend knowledge-based and time-serving learning programmes and to avoid paper based assessment regimes' (Ecclestone 1997: 300).

There is a great deal in common between NVQs and the older training. For example, both see learning as an individual process and both give little emphasis to general or theoretical knowledge. However, the role of the teacher or trainer is somewhat different in each. In non-NVQ training, the role of teacher or trainer is one of knowledge and skill transmission. NVQs however, are independent of process both in terms of content and time, focusing only on outcomes (Burke 1994). The teachers of vocationally specific courses of the NVQ type remain relatively agnostic about the teaching and learning method, as it is outcomes and performance that they consider to be important (Jessup 1991). In NVQ training the role of the 'teacher' shifts to that of assessor, with the teacher verifying whether a candidate can demonstrate their workplace 'competence' which is precisely specified.

General vocational education

The tradition of general vocational education is complex and encompasses a didactic 'training' approach on one extreme and getting learners to 'do things' with the teacher acting as a guide or facilitator on the other. It contains within it a number of different developments, reflecting FE colleges' traditional links with industry and the world of work (Avis 1990); its newer interface with schools; and its role in providing programmes for the unemployed. General vocational education represents a range of vocationally orientated curricular developments that were the result of debates about education in the 1970s and early 1980s (Lee *et al.* 2003). The three main foci of the debate concerned, first, the purposes and practices of the school curriculum and how it had lost touch with the world of work (Callaghan 1976); second, growing anxiety at the collapse of the youth labour market (Gleeson 1990); and, third, the growing awareness concerning the weakness of existing vocational courses.

Because of the complexity of the general vocational tradition I make three analytic distinctions in the discussion that follows: 'new vocationalism'; 'pre-vocationalism and 'general vocationalism'.[7]

New vocationalism came into existence as a response to the growing youth unemployment of the late 1970s and 1980s, and the increasing realisation that existing provision was inadequate for training young people for the new labour market. Based upon this premise, courses such as the Youth Opportunities Programme (YOPS) started in the late 1970s, leading to the more ambitious Youth Training Scheme (YTS) in 1983. YTS was intended to be a modernised apprenticeship, committed to providing places for all 16- and 17-year-old school leavers who were out of work in order to enhance their 'employability'. These early developments in new vocational courses were caught between the need to do something about youth unemployment and the need to develop a genuine training route (Ainley and Corney 1990). The programmes were not designed to be occupationally specific and gave priority to personal and social skills (Ainley 1990). Many of the new vocational courses were based upon a dual notion of work experience combined with the inculcation of work/life skills (MSC 1982) or 'life preparation skills' (Pring 1995) which were transferable from one occupation to another. This involved a redefinition of vocational skills, often referred to as 'life skills', with attention increasingly being paid to the improvement of a young person's 'personal and coping skills' (Stoney and Lines 1987), thus making explicit what was implicit in other courses for lower achieving students destined for low-skill jobs in a changing labour market. In general, 'preparation for work' on these schemes meant remedial help for those seeking mainly low-paid, unskilled employment (Esland 1996).

New vocationalism is not a clear-cut teaching and learning tradition; it is one that borrows from a number of other approaches and thus crosses pedagogic boundaries. On the other hand there is a great deal of variation in the delivery of courses and there has been a number of local innovations in new vocationalism that have been experimental and creative. New vocational courses have had many critics (Bates *et al.* 1984; Dale 1985; Ainley 1988; Gleeson 1990), who have claimed that such schemes are a means of getting young people to lower their expectations and to socialise them into 'knowing their place', as well as being a source of cheap labour for employers. However, the situation was more complex than this, because new vocationalism and many of the teaching and learning techniques employed represented a genuine criticism of existing curricula. New vocationalism set a challenge for pedagogy regarding how students learn in a workplace context, the extent to which such learning can be transferred to other contexts and the way in which college learning can mediate such a transfer.

The second distinction within the tradition of general vocational qualifications is that of pre-vocationalism. Pre-vocationalism both arose from the 'Great Education Debate' (Callaghan 1976), which accused the existing school curriculum of being out of touch with the world of work, and also represented a response by the DES to youth unemployment. This, according to Raggatt and Williams (1999), was intended to prevent the MSC from further encroaching on DES territory. The aim of pre-vocationalism was to provide a curriculum for those who opted to stay on in full-time education but who could not achieve through the academic route and were vocationally undecided. The Certificate of Pre-Vocational Education (CPVE) had a concept of vocationalism which extended beyond the 'skills for jobs' emphasis of new vocational courses (Ecclestone 1997). CPVE, unlike YTS, was divided into a core of ten subjects, such as numeracy and information technology, as well as specified vocational studies.

The development of pre-vocational courses was stimulated by the Technical and Vocational Education Initiative (TVEI). This was a scheme to help equip young people between the ages of 14 and 18 for working life by increasing the relevance of technical and vocational aspects of secondary schools (Finegold and Soskice 1988) through categorical funding. TVEI did not develop into establishing low-level vocational courses as many predicted in the early stages (Gleeson and Smith 1987). Once schools and colleges had received TVEI funds, there was a great deal of local innovation enabling schools and colleges to install computers and provide in-service training for teachers to use them. Craft, design and technology replaced older more traditional subjects; work experience and visits were included in courses; and modularisation was developed to include broader more vocational and technical issues.

These pre-vocational courses adopted an approach to pedagogy which emphasised learning as a process; the student would be actively involved in applying knowledge. Furthermore, pre-vocational courses stressed guidance and support for students, with the pedagogic role of the teacher being that of guide or facilitator. A key pre-vocational pedagogic instrument was the assignment, which emphasised the active role of the learner. Assignments were pioneered in CPVE, BTEC and DVE programmes and formalised later in GNVQs (Wyatt 1995). The learning process was based on students collecting evidence of activity, which was then checked against the assessment specification and put together in a portfolio for submission. The teaching and learning of CPVE and BTEC general courses were based on a rejection of academic models of knowledge transmission associated with subject teaching which, by implication, were only appropriate for the highest achievers (Young and Lucas 1999). Pre-vocational courses emphasised the active involvement of students in their own learning and stressed the crucial importance of what the learner is 'doing' (Harkin 1995). Knowledge was not related to subjects, but to its application, which, alongside a concept of 'core skills', distinguishes the pre-vocational from the NVQ (Spours 1995a).

A third distinction within the tradition of general vocational qualifications is the General National Vocational Qualification (GNVQ) that developed in the early 1990s and drew upon the experience of new vocational and pre-vocational courses such as CPVE and BTEC. Many GNVQs have now been replaced by 'vocational A levels' or 'vocational GCSEs' following the Curriculum 2000 developments (Hodgson and Spours 2003). However, they still represent an important tradition of teaching and learning in FE colleges. The development of GNVQs was brought about by the NCVQ and was designed as a set of qualifications that constituted an alternative to general education and vocationally specific courses, designed to lead to employment or higher education.[8] GNVQs drew on the traditions of vocationally specific qualifications teaching 'key skills' and academic knowledge through application.[9] For example, mathematics became the 'application of number' and English became 'communication'. The establishment of GNVQs also contained a reaction to the rigidities of traditional academic approaches (Lau-Walker 1995). GNVQs adopted an assignment-based approach where learning becomes a process of gathering and evaluating evidence (Young and Lucas 1999).

Teaching and learning within GNVQs showed diversity, although Harkin (1995) suggests that it was predominantly activity-based with great emphasis being given to supporting learners through guidance, setting targets and encouraging independent learning, and using different communication styles and teaching methods from those used in A levels and GCSEs. Harkin's research found that GNVQ classes had higher levels of student activity and less passive learning. He found that some-times it was the more experienced A-level teachers who found it difficult to adopt a more interpersonal teaching style.

It has been suggested, however, that due to the absence of course syl-labuses for GNVQs there was an over-concentration on assessment (Spours 1995a) and a large amount of time spent on verification (Capey 1995). In other words, teachers focused on the collection of evidence to satisfy the density of competence criteria, sometimes at the expense of broader knowledge (Hyland 1994) which is not taught separately but 'embedded' in the process of application. Concerns have also been expressed that the GNVQ assessment criteria created a mechanism for substantive regulation over assessment, quality assurance and awarding bodies (Ecclestone 2000). Concerns have also been expressed of the dan-ger of losing specialism, whether academic or vocational in the new generic applied route, where key skills are a poor substitute for a good general education (Green 1997).

Much has changed in the last few years with the growth of vocational GCSEs and Advanced Vocational Certificates in Education (AVCEs) in which key skills have been uncoupled and made free standing. These changes have been introduced with the intention of giving parity of esteem with academic qualifications. Recent research (Savory *et al.* 2003) suggests, however, that the increasing academic approach to assessment in AVCEs has resulted in a return to traditional teacher-centred delivery and also high drop-out rates on these new courses. Many teachers are now considering the defunct GNVQ advanced courses as more suited to the needs of their less 'academic' learners (Ecclestone 2002) because they were more practice-focused and assessed in a less formal way (Brooks and Lucas 2004). It is still early in the development of these new qualifications to judge their long-term effect.

Adult and community education

Although FE colleges have been providing certain types of vocational and certificated adult education and training for many years, community adult education has been until recently quite autonomous from FE colleges and provided by adult education institutes (AEIs). Following incorporation in 1993, however, the new FEFC funding regime forced many traditional AEI courses into FE colleges, thus including yet another tradition within the FE college sector.

Adult and community education claims many ideological roots, from Plato to Rousseau, to Ivan Illich (1973). Many child-centred educational theorists such as Dewey (1938) have influenced practitioners to believe that education should not be passive, but should be an active and inter-active process that empowers the individual. Dialogue, empowerment, student-centred learning and negotiation are all more or less the vocabu-lary of this tradition of education (Long 1990). Adult education is also associated with a reaction against the schooling model of pedagogy, which some adult educators believe is equally as bad in colleges of FE.

What distinguishes adult education from traditional school pedagogy is the criticism that subject-based general education and traditional voca-tional education tend to neglect what learners bring to the college. As a result many skills that adults bring to FE are not given formal recogni-tion (Jarvis 1983). This argument has led to the movement that allows prior knowledge to be accredited and assessed against existing courses.

Another interpretation of adult education stems from the recognition of life experience as a base upon which further learning should be built, rather than upon external existing knowledge. This is the basis of andra-gogy. The argument is taken to an extreme by the followers of Martin Knowles (1980, 1985) who argue that any kind of pedagogy inevitably underplays the self-direction that has to be the underlying principle of adult learning. On this basis, Knowles argues that drawing upon prior experience moves the adult learner from being a dependent person to one that is self-directed. Self-directed learning leads not only to a question-ing of the learner's social place and role but also to a shift in orientation from subject-centred learning to problem-centred learning.

A similar approach is that of Paulo Freire (1970), whose educational philosophy starts from his idea that education must be located in the material reality of relevance to the individual. In his discussion of the teaching of literacy, he proposes that this should start with a study of people's lives, of their reality in all its contradictions, which serves as the basis upon which to build words and concepts.

Both Freire and Knowles have had a considerable influence on adult educators, reinforcing adult education's traditional hostility to schooling while at the same time corresponding to their traditional radical political agenda (Evans 1987). The role of the 'teacher', as in the pre-vocational tradition referred to earlier, is primarily involved in keeping students active, doing things, acting as a facilitator and coach (Brookfield 1986). This has led to seeing a 'teacher' as a facilitator and friend in order to promote autonomous learning, encouraging learners to define their own learning goals and to help individuals understand how they learn best.

There is much to be said for the adult and community tradition, particularly concerning the recognition of learner's previous experience, of building self-directed active learning (Roland 1991), and of accrediting prior learning. The problem with the approach adopted by many supporters of andragogy is that they convert a criticism of the weakness of schooling and training models into a complete alternative approach to teaching and learning (Young and Lucas 1999). Andragogy with its stress on self-directedness denies the importance of external authority or knowledge, and an uncritical celebration of personal experience can all too easily ignore the importance of providing learners with a knowledge base or theoretical ideas for reflecting on that experience (Usher and Edwards 1994). This not only neglects certain basic features of any learning, whatever the age, but also seems to make the dubious suggestion that prior experience is what distinguishes adult learning from childhood learning.

This is not to argue that a learner's prior experience (often neglected in schools and FE colleges) is not an important basis to enhancing learning. Prior experience is crucial for any learners beginning a course in FE. However, the informal experiential knowledge that people acquire in the pre-college experience, while very important, should only be a partial basis for adopting a particular pedagogic approach (Young and Lucas 1999).

Adult basic skills

This teaching and learning tradition has until recently been largely hidden within adult and community education. However, in 1999 the Moser Report highlighted two major issues that moved adult basic skills teaching to the top of the educational agenda, attracting a lot of reform, resources and political significance. The Moser Report highlighted very low levels of literacy and numeracy in the adult population at a time when there was increasing concern over the government's agenda of social inclusion. The report also found that the teaching of basic skills in literacy, numeracy and ESOL was weak. It found no clear structure, content or level to the multitude of courses that was offered in these areas. Furthermore, many teachers of adult literacy, numeracy and ESOL lacked teaching and specialist qualifications and knowledge.[10]

In response to these findings, a national 'core curriculum' for the teaching of literacy, numeracy and ESOL was developed and made obligatory for the first time in the post-compulsory sector. In addition, new teachers of numeracy, literacy and ESOL were required to meet both the FENTO teaching standards and achieve a level 4 subject knowledge based upon subject specifications introduced by the Adult Basic Skills Strategy Unit (ABSSU). These subject specifications define the knowledge, personal skills and understanding required of teachers of adult literacy, numeracy and ESOL.[11]

The effect of what is, in essence, a national curriculum in these three areas is difficult to assess, particularly as each subject area has its own subject sub-cultures and traditions; ESOL, for example, is separate from literacy and TESOL. For teacher education in the university sector these changes present challenges for traditional approaches to initial teacher education because they represent a shift from the normal assumption that student teachers have subject/vocational knowledge before coming onto the programme. Teaching subject knowledge alongside pedagogy is new in FE teacher education and the effects it will have on the teaching and learning of literacy, numeracy and ESOL are difficult to predict since both the core curriculum and the subject specifications are still in the early stages of implementation (Lucas *et al*. 2004). What is clear is that recent developments in adult basic skills are challenging old ideas and assumptions; a new teaching and learning tradition is beginning to emerge.

Special educational needs

Provision for students with special educational needs (SEN) is relatively new to FE; following patchy provision in the 1970s there has been rapid growth in the last 15 years (Bradley *et al*. 1994; FEFC 1996b). Since FE college incorporation the provision for students with SEN has moved from the periphery to the mainstream (Macadam and Sutcliffe 1996). It has been claimed that this was because SEN was separately funded by the FEFC (Dee 1999).[12]

There is a vast literature concerning the education of students with SEN, although most of the discussion and research has focused upon the school sectors. Therefore provision of special educational needs in FE has raised many of the same issues that have been debated for schools. These include definitions of special educational needs and also whether SEN provision should be integrated within mainstream schools and colleges or be provided in separate institutions (Wedell 1993). Such issues have raised important questions. For example, do individuals with learning difficulties require additional teaching of the same kind, or is there a different kind of teaching or pedagogy that is required (Corbett and Norwich 1999)?[13]

The idea of inclusive learning derives from a socially constructed model of disability in which the barriers faced by disabled people are created by society rather than from an individual's disability. This approach found a voice in FE in an FEFC report, *Inclusive Learning* (FEFC 1996b), which highlighted the importance of the learning process, stressing the need for educational institutions to meet the individual's learning need, not to focus on the individual's learning difficulties as though these were some sort of deficit. Inclusive learning, according to the FEFC report, takes place when there is the greatest match or fit between the provision made and the individual learner's needs, which implies that changes need to take place in the learning context to meet students' needs, rather than individuals fitting into existing arrangements (Dee 1999). The teaching and learning implications of taking such an approach are significant, as teachers will need to identify and accommodate individual needs and adopt individual learning styles as appropriate.

Notions of inclusive learning, unlike earlier approaches to SEN, stress the importance of context. In other words, the argument is that even the traditional definition of learning difficulties, which has focused on individual deficits, is more to do with the context of learning than was previously thought. This has shifted the debate concerning the teaching of those with SEN or other learning difficulties from an individual 'deficit model' to one which examines a college's practices and ethos, stressing individual needs within a context or 'community of practice' (Lave 1993).

Tutoring and guidance

This is a difficult tradition to identify as it has so many aims and purposes. Yet it has had an important influence on the professional practice of FE teachers (Watts 1990). For example, it can be used as a means of managing the student, of enhancing the educational process or of simply providing specific forms of guidance, such as careers guidance. Curriculum developments discussed above, such as YTS, CPVE, and initiatives like TVEI, led to FE teachers taking on a greater tutoring and guidance role. Tutoring and guidance, such as providing individual learning support and individual target setting are also central to the teaching and learning approach adopted by GNVQs, other general vocational qualifications and many other traditional academic courses (FEU 1994).

The FEFC funding regime in FE also gave emphasis to pre-entry and entry guidance which is specifically funded and audited (Lucas 1999), and the growth of adult returners to FE colleges has meant that accreditation of prior learning is becoming an increasing responsibility of the FE teacher (Payne and Edwards 1996). Tutoring and guidance have also become particularly relevant for the FE college teacher within the context of improving retention and progression, and enhancing lifelong learning (NIACE 1998). This requires new approaches and skills on the part of the FE college teacher, as new learners now receive pre-course guidance, support in action planning, establishing a learning contract, ongoing guidance, review of learning, and formative assessment (Lanigan 1994).

One example of the growing use of tutoring and guidance is the movement towards 'formative value added' (Spours and Hodgson 1996), which uses value-added data as a means of setting realistic learning targets and raising student achievement. This requires a rigorous tutoring and guidance system designed to focus students on their strengths and weaknesses, and raise student aspirations by developing the individual's capacity for managing their own learning. Another example is developments in general vocational, adult and community education where distance, open and flexible learning stresses the importance of 'supported self study'. This in turn gives a greater emphasis to supervising, counselling and guidance skills with the 'teacher' acting as coach, facilitator, and mentor (Edwards 1993).

Little research exists in the area of tutoring and guidance in FE colleges, where it often represents not a separate tradition but more a development alongside many courses and practices. The FE college teacher now provides individual learning support, sets learning targets and action plans, acts as tutor, supervisor and mentor, accredits prior learning, gives pastoral care and monitors progress (Kerry and Tollitt-Evans 1992). The effect of this has been in some circumstances to blur the role of the FE college teacher between teacher and tutor (Edwards 1993). The emphasis given to tutoring/guidance raises issues about whether it is possible to describe this practice as 'pedagogy of guidance' (Lucas 1996). In other words, does something pedagogically different take place in this learning process that distinguishes it from teaching a class or group?

Distance, open and flexible learning

This relatively new tradition in FE colleges is important because it represents an aspect of meeting the diverse needs of FE learners and of providing more flexible provision. It is linked to the growing use of tutoring and guidance, discussed above, and is having an effect on the practice of many FE college teachers as they adopt more learner-centred and flexible approaches to teaching and learning (Wilmot and McLean 1994). The movement towards more open and distance learning, combined with developments in information and computer technology, opens up a potential for flexibility that allows people to learn in unconventional ways (Bates 1995).

The precursors of these practices emerged from outside FE colleges in the form of correspondence courses and the developments that arose from the Open University and the adult education movement (Jarvis 1995). Distance learning implies the separation of the teacher and learner for much of the learning process, distinguishing it from face-to-face education. It also implies the use of learning materials and technology (Longworth and Davis 1996) and a two-way traffic of written work and learning materials between tutors and students, who spend the overwhelming majority of their time working on their own. It includes learning workshops, drop-in learning centres, resource-based learning, on-line access and all uses of information and communication technologies.

Much like the use of information and communication technology, issues concerning the implications for teaching and learning are often not given priority, and flexible learning, like other approaches outlined above, can become a dogma or a fad that fails to consider pedagogic techniques according to their fitness for purpose (Young and Lucas 1999). There is evidence that resource-based approaches on their own are not appropriate for many FE students, who lack the motivation, confidence and skills to learn independently (Guile and Hayton 1999). They are used without considering what is appropriate for independent study and what is best learnt in a group involving discussion and interaction. Student learning is often assumed to take place with the production of learning packs, visits to open learning centres or access to computers, with little consideration being given to new forms of learning, the context of learning, or learning with others. It has been suggested that the growing use of open and flexible learning techniques, combined with the use of more tutoring and guidance, does not diminish the role of the teacher but does imply a re-evaluation of teaching and learning methods and the practice of the FE teacher (Guile and Hayton 1999).

Conclusion

The factors that distinguish FE from schools and universities are its vocational roots and the ever-growing diversity of learners. As the chapter has shown, FE colleges are institutions where a number of different teaching and learning traditions confront each other – some reflecting FE's vocational past, others reflecting newer, school or adult education traditions (Young and Lucas 1999). Each teaching and learning tradition has importance in meeting the diverse learning needs and destinations of those coming to FE.

In practice, there are contested views and overlap within and between teaching and learning traditions. However, despite the provisional nature of the eight categories described above they do illuminate the fragmented nature and diversity of teaching and learning in FE, and are useful for analysing the diverse practices of FE practitioners. These diverse practices are examined further in the next chapter in a discussion of the practices of the FE teacher through four conceptual models.

Notes

1 Although as Higham *et al.* (1996) point out, some A levels are breaking down subject divisions and relevance to the workplace, for example the A level in Business, Media and Theatre Studies.

2 This tradition lumps general education courses together, yet there is variety within this category. Unwin (1997) shows in her research that students on Modern Apprenticeships said that A level represented a return to didactic teaching, whereas GCSEs had been more student-focused, with teachers using a variety of teaching and learning strategies.

3 The teacher-centred, subject knowledge 'transmission' mode of teaching could however be applied to much of the training that takes place on vocational courses, particularly day-release and HNCs/Ds. Very little research has been done on these courses.

4 The didactic approach to teaching subject-focused, general and decontextualised knowledge reflects syllabuses which assume that there is a straightforward relationship between a model of teaching as 'knowledge transmission' and a model of learning as the 'acquisition of knowledge' (Young and Lucas 1999).

5 Bloomer records how one of the students (Matt) he interviewed was repeatedly told by his tutors 'not to incorporate knowledge from other subjects' (Bloomer 1997: 134).

6 Raggat and Williams (1999) suggest that in fact employers did not participate very much and most of the competencies and standards were driven by NCVQ officials.

7 In using these three distinctions it is worth noting that courses such as BTEC National and BTEC Higher qualifications do not feature. Gleeson (1989) places BTEC National, HNDs and other higher level general vocational courses together with academic courses in a category of 'academic technical qualifications', assuming that all require academic competence. This makes a distinction between lower level general vocational education such as BTEC general and higher level vocational education courses for technical administrative and relatively privileged non-manual work (Ainley 1990).

8 Williams (1999) argues, however, that these were for the less 'able' and were directed towards students who were less academic.

9 The terms 'core skills' and 'key skills' are used interchangeably.

10 This statement by the report was made despite the fact that in both ESOL and literacy a number of well established specialist qualifications already existed.

11 Guidance on the specialist pedagogical aspects of each area was published separately later on.

12 Discussed in chapter 2.

13 This question can equally be applied to all individual learning needs and could lead to the question: are not some teaching methods or pedagogies more suited to some students than others whatever their abilities or difficulties?

9 Models for understanding the practices of FE teachers

Introduction

This chapter explores four conceptual models to help understand the diverse practices of FE teachers. Although the four models do not describe all the diverse practices of FE teachers, they do represent the main approaches used in ITE and staff development programmes.

The 'vocational specialist' and the 'competent practitioner' connect together as models that mainly apply to vocational FE teachers. The 'subject specialist' and the 'reflective practitioner' are taken together because they represent models applied to FE teachers on academic programmes. In other words the models reflect continuing academic and vocational divisions and traditions.

The vocational specialist

In the technical colleges of the 1970s, teaching was traditionally associated with 'training' and the transmission of a craft or technical knowledge to technicians and day-release students; little emphasis was given to broader knowledge or underlying rationale. Chapter 4 described how the majority of technical teachers were drawn directly from industry and had little opportunity for teacher training. Furthermore, until very recently no statutory qualification was required to teach in FE, reflecting the view that vocational/technical expertise and experience were adequate for teaching – a view strongly reinforced by vocational teachers themselves.

According to Tipton (1973), departments in colleges tended to reflect the values and culture of the industry; staff were often divided by the physical layout of the buildings, and the college structures and college culture tended to reflect these different cultures.

Craftsmen taught students who were to become craftsman, graduates taught students who would go to university and so on. The formal structure of the college, therefore invited staff to feel different from one another rather than alike.

(Tipton 1973: x)

In her study of teachers, Venables noted attitudes towards teaching in technical colleges in the 1950 and 1960s:

For most of them pride in their skill as engineers, scientists or craftsmen took precedence over any pride in pedagogy. ... There was no spontaneous reference by any member of staff to an interest in the art of teaching as such or in examining in any depth the learning problems of their students. A few were beginning (in 1963) to take an interest in teaching machines,[1] but on the whole actual proposals for change met with pronounced inertia.

(Venables 1967: 220)

Gleeson and Mardle (1980) also found that vocational teachers had very strong identities as trainers, not teachers. They were of the view that only those with specific industrial or craft experience should or could teach students from that particular industry. Perhaps as a result the content of courses tended to focus on narrow industry-specific skills at the expense of other more general skills that could be used for other tasks or employment (Sheldrake and Vickerstaff 1987). Classroom authority was founded upon their industrial experience and the fact that they 'had served their time' and were well placed to pass on the know-how to those 'who also want their ticket'.

Even though colleges had changed from technical to further education colleges (see chapter 1) in the 1970s and 1980s, the culture of the 'old technical teacher' still maintained a strong presence, particularly in vocational departments. Despite all the changes introduced by the NCVQ (see below) and the changes in further education colleges over the past three decades or so (Green and Lucas 1999), the legacy continued into the 1990s of the vocational teacher seeing industrial and trade expertise as a sufficient qualification to teach (Young *et al.* 1995).[2] Until the mid- to late 1980s, the concept of the 'vocational specialist' was the only model for the professional practice for vocational subject teachers, even though the practice remained entrenched within the traditions and cultures of their craft and industrial backgrounds.

The emergence of 'standards' and competence in vocational qualification

Historically, vocational qualifications, like technical education in general, were characterised by a *laissez-faire* attitude on the part of the government, or the 'play of market forces' (Stringer and Richardson 1982). The training of apprentices was assumed to be the business of industry and had nothing to do with government (Sheldrake and Vickerstaff 1987). It was not until the 1962 White Paper *Industrial Training: Government proposals* and the subsequent Industrial Training Act in 1964 that a change in government policy took place, signalling 'the arrival of a new consensus behind a more interventionist approach to training policy' (Raggatt and Williams 1999: 7). This interventionist approach reflected the growing concern that training methods were out-of-date, too narrowly focused upon specific industries and reinforced restrictive practices maintained by the trade unions (Donovan Commission 1968).

Arising from the Donovan Report, the Employment and Training Act of 1973 established a national training agency, which it was claimed would co-ordinate the work of the Industrial Training Boards (ITBs) and forecast skill changes and skill shortages. This agency became known as the Manpower Services Commission (MSC). In May 1981, within the context of a sharp rise in unemployment, the MSC formulated its New Training Initiative (NTI). The NTI proposed to give young people 'agreed standards of skills appropriate to the jobs available and to provide them with a basis for progress to further learning' (MSC 1981: 4). By the time of the MSC's demise in 1987 it had changed the *laissez-faire* policy regarding education and training in general, and vocational qualifications in particular, to a strong interventionist policy by establishing standards based upon an idea of occupational competence.

In the 1980s, the Conservative government (influenced by the MSC) argued that a national qualifications framework was required to raise the status of vocational qualifications. The White Paper *Working Together –*

Education and training (ED/DES 1986) reinforced the need to establish standards and led to the formation of the National Council for Vocational Qualifications (NCVQ). The task set for the NCVQ was to secure standards of occupational competence for vocational qualifications within a new national framework of comprehensive standards of competency for all occupational sectors set by employers.

As with formation of the MSC, there was initially broad support for the NCVQ (Sutton 1992), with many FE colleges and other organisations such as NIACE (1990) seeing many advantages in the NCVQ model. Some supported the council because of its rationalisation of the 'qualification jungle'. It was felt that the introduction of a competence-based approach and the unitisation of learning would facilitate more flexible courses, routes and progression pathways, and learners would be motivated because of the transparency of standards and outcomes (Jessup 1991).

Some impetus for the move towards standards and competencies came from those who felt education should be made more relevant to the employers' interests. It is, however, too easy to attribute the emergence of the NVQ framework to a right-wing trend: 'its origins are much more complex including a radical critique from the left and a slide in confidence on the part of many committed educationalists in the ability of the educational system to deliver opportunities for more disadvantaged young people' (Raggatt and Williams 1999: 24). From both the left and right of the political spectrum the view was put forward that 'organised education' had got it wrong, taught the wrong things and did not measure and assess what it should (Wolf 1995).[3] For the radical right these changes constituted a political and ideological critique of the 'education industry' and represented an extension of control over so-called professional expertise (Jones and Moore 1993). For many taking a more leftist stance, the 'transparency' of narrow competence-based NVQs was in contrast to the opaqueness and elitism of traditional academic assessment (Jessup 1991). It was this critique of traditional training practices and the inadequacy of general education from both the left and the right of the political spectrum that led to the growing trend towards defining 'competence' and 'standards' against which the quality of training could be measured and assessed.

The emergence of the 'competent practitioner'

Unlike in other educational sectors, the impetus to reform vocational qualifications in the UK was the dominant influence in the application of standards and competencies to teachers in further education colleges. Standards and competence developed in relation to training in industry and then to 'vocational specialists' in FE colleges. When standards and competence were applied to the implicit model of the vocational teacher as 'vocational specialist', a more explicit model was created upon which to define the practice of FE teachers. Such a model might be described as the 'competent practitioner'.

The idea of the 'competent practitioner' in FE was also strengthened by the 'benign neglect' of FE teacher development (Young *et al.* 1995), the relative absence of any other explicit model of professionalism (Robson 1998), and the closeness of the FE college sector to employment and industrial models of working and training cultures. This was particularly true of 'vocational specialists', who were in favour of a model that saw practitioners as technicians or experts who trained in the apprenticeship model. If teaching is seen as training or, as Hodkinson (1995) argues, if education and training in FE is seen through an 'industrial metaphor', quality and competence are instrumental and technical, and their primary use is as a tool for measuring effectiveness and efficiency in order to control and regulate employees (Mahony and Hextall 2000).

Within this context, competence-based education and training (CBET) was gradually introduced into a number of initial and in-service courses for FE college teachers during the 1980s, aided by the former Further Education Unit (FEU 1992) with its work on standards developed by the Training and Development Lead Body (TDLB). The TDLB was established in 1990 to develop cross-sector standards applying to training and development. While it was originally concerned with instruction and supervision of training (Chown 1992), it also developed a range of competencies to cover teaching, assessing, management roles and staff development in the FE sector (see chapter 6). Teacher assessment was carried out with reference to the TDLB standards and presented in a portfolio of various kinds of evidence, such as reports, memos, lesson plans, etc., which were then authenticated to see if they matched the standards.

The development and use of TDLB standards not only influenced ITE FE courses in universities, but also other college-based initial teacher training provision, such as the City and Guild 730 series of certificates. By the early 1990s, the City and Guilds was offering a 7306 scheme which recognised and embodied the TDLB standards assessor awards as well as the Internal Verifier Award (D34). By the early 1990s, the trend for teacher training and professional development programmes to be competence-based seemed to sweeping the field.

While the model of the 'competent practitioner' gained ground, criticisms of the competence-based approach grew. A major criticism was that it did not give enough scope for knowledge and understanding (Wolf 1989) and was therefore not applicable to teacher education (Hyland 1994). Another area of debate and disagreement was whether occupational competence and standards should be given a broad or narrow focus. In other words, whether they should focus on broad occupational roles that include knowledge and understanding, or routine aspects of work activity (Mansfield 1989). Even those who agreed that having statements of competence were a good way forward could not agree on who should set the standards, let alone on the definition of competency (Ashworth 1993).

The collection of evidence of existing practice (which may be a good thing for some purposes) is quite a different process from learning and professional development. This is because it is a process of verification of individualised practice within the specific programme areas and where professional development relies upon evidence collection (Hodkinson 1998). The individualistic nature of learning reinforces the insularity of professional practice (Ecclestone 2002) and does not enhance teaching and learning to meet the diverse needs of the FE college learner (Bathmaker 1999). TDLB units and competence-based training programmes were developed for the 'vocational specialist' delivering NVQ programmes using the more explicit concept of the 'competent practitioner'.[4] This model came to dominate initial training and staff development programmes in the 1990s and remains an influential model upon which FE teachers are judged.

The 'competent practitioner' and university-based ITE courses

During the 1990s, some universities modelled or 'mapped' their courses against TDLB standards, adopting an NVQ structure and providing accreditation of prior learning (APL) for the TDLB standards towards their award. Some redesigned their courses on the NCVQ model even calling for 'product evidence' in their assessment (Maynard 1995). Some used broad competencies akin to those used by the TTA, whilst others 'subverted' the NVQ approach to include knowledge and understanding.

The interpretation of competencies in ITE showed great variety; for example, some universities adopted a functional analysis 'tick box' approach only in the first phase of the teacher education programmes. This meant embracing the idea of the 'competent practitioner' in the first phase and moving on to a reflective practitioner model in the second phase. In a survey carried out in the late 1990s of 21 colleges and 27 universities all of the respondents claimed that they incorporated some aspects of competence-based assessments and more than 50 per cent were completely competence-based (UPDC 1999).[5] There can be little doubt that in the early to mid-1990s there was a concerted effort to make teacher education competence-based (Lee *et al.* 2003).

Part of the appeal of competence-based approaches to FE ITE and staff development programmes derived from the fact that it corresponded to a sort of common sense (Ecclestone 1995, 1997). Who could argue against student teachers knowing exactly what they have to do and how they will be assessed? Why not base teacher training on an analysis of the known competencies of skilled and experienced FE teachers (Renolds 1999)? The need for defined practical know-how coincided with the wishes of many beginning teachers (Ecclestone 1997). The central idea that one should look at what people do and compare a candidate's performance with an independent definition of what can be achieved is appealing and many people do not understand why it cannot be done.

It is difficult to avoid some use of standards in teacher education. There are after all some common features between initial teacher education courses and workplace learning (Fuller and Unwin 2002). A large part of the course is based in the workplace (school or college). Passing and failing is based in a large part upon observation of practical teaching. While written tests are always a part of the assessment, nobody qualifies who is not considered competent in the classroom. What is considered to be competent practice is often based upon a joint assessment of college (employer) and university. In many cases, employer (college) involvement is increasing with some courses being completely work-based. Reliable research concerning the effects of the variety of ways in which standards and competency has been applied is yet to be done. Although there are national standards there is still no clear consensus in the interpretation of competency, level or standards when applied to FE ITE (see chapters 6 and 7). Some courses use broader definitions of competencies that emphasise knowledge and independent judgement and there is a variety of ways of using standards (Lucas *et al.* 2004). Perhaps, as chapter 7 suggests, the big division lies between industrial occupational standards and professional standards.

The FE teacher as 'subject specialist'

The graduate 'subject specialist' teacher is a relatively new entrant to the FE sector. The number of graduates in FE colleges rose from 9,719 in 1962 to 24,463 in 1976 (DES 1976), making up over one-third of full-time teaching staff.

In examining the model of the FE teacher as a 'subject specialist', research from outside the FE sector will be drawn upon. Outside FE research on the identity and practice of teachers and their subject knowledge has focused largely on the secondary school sector,[6] although some work has been carried out with university teachers (Becher 1989). There is relatively little research conducted on the teaching of general education in FE colleges; that said, both teaching and professional traditions from schools and universities are arguably of increasing relevance to the FE college sector.

In a study of secondary school teachers Ferguson and Womak (1993) suggest that the model of the teacher as 'subject specialist' forms a strong part of a teacher's identity. As a result individuals come to see themselves not so much as teachers in general but more as subject specialists. Those undertaking initial teacher preparation (particularly within secondary school ITE programmes) found that learning to teach took place largely within different subject departments (Widen and Grimmett 1995). This often reinforced subject cultures or sub-cultures, which reflected common understandings about teaching and learning (Hargreaves 1994). In turn these subject cultures were reflected in general education departments in FE colleges, perpetuating different subject-based attitudes to teaching and learning (FEFC 1999b).

Becher (1989), in a study of university teachers, describes different disciplinary groups as 'academic tribes', who represent distinctive cultures, linguistic forms and beliefs which are often quite hostile caricatures of colleagues in other subject areas. In addition to this, university teachers were not found by Becher to be committed to the university as a whole but rather to their subject and department. The subject was the major influence on their teaching methods or pedagogical beliefs and interpretation of curriculum (Van Driel *et al.* 1997).

The importance of subject knowledge to teachers has been much debated, often taking the form of a dichotomous argument between those who assert that subject matter knowledge is the most important factor positively affecting teaching quality (Ball and McDiarmid 1990), and those who argue that pedagogic knowledge is more important and that an over concentration on subject expertise on its own does not make a good teacher in that subject (Venman 1984).[7] In research into teacher training for teachers of adult language, literacy and numeracy similar problems concerning the content and balance between subject knowledge and teaching knowledge were encountered (Lucas *et al.* 2004). The research found that in meeting the diverse needs of learners, the relationship between subject knowledge and pedagogic knowledge was a major question that determined the success of the programmes. The problem faced by the course developers was how to bring the two types of knowledge (subject knowledge and pedagogic knowledge) together in ways that enhance practice. This is a fundamental pedagogic problem that all teacher educators face – namely that of relating theory and practice.

The 'subject specialist' teacher in FE colleges is traditionally associated with the teaching of GCSEs and A levels or, more recently, access courses to university (Young and Lucas 1999). In practice, many FE teachers who would formerly have been teaching A levels are now more likely to be required to embrace new programmes. There is a growing overlap between teaching and learning that cuts across subject boundaries, as many subject specialists in FE colleges now teach on more than one type of programme (Simmons 1999), particularly in general vocational programmes (Harkin 1995). Furthermore, the changing contexts in which FE teachers work, particularly the growth of general vocational qualifications and initiatives such as Curriculum 2000, emphasise the importance of broader knowledge and key skills.

This is not to suggest that the boundaries between subjects are easy to overcome in FE colleges. Subject-specific knowledge cannot be shared by all members of the profession. Most FE colleges are large and diverse, accommodating a wide variety of specialisms and cultures and this diversity of specialism is the strength of the FE college sector. As is argued below, specialist knowledge has a double-edged significance. It is an important strength in meeting the diverse needs of FE students, yet the subject specialist FE teacher who sees their subject as completely separate from others, erects barriers and restricts opportunities for teachers and students to learn from one another. Furthermore, as chapter 8 illustrates, the teaching of subjects, whether vocational or academic, tends to be based upon predominantly individualistic assumptions about the nature of learning (Young and Lucas, 1999), failing to find what Shulman (1986) describes as the blend between the content and process of teaching. This is not to suggest that knowledge of the subject matter being taught is not important. There is clearly a relationship between how something is taught and the knowledge the person teaching it possesses (Watkins and Mortimore 1999). It has, however, been argued that the FE practitioner who sees him or herself primarily as subject specialist can become entrenched in attitudes and practices, which makes it difficult to create a consensus around a body of professional knowledge and identity shared with other practitioners.

The emergence of the 'reflective practitioner'

Research carried out during the early 1980s concerning the initial training of secondary school teachers (HMI 1983) showed that ITE programmes offered by universities primarily focused upon the teaching of the student's subject specialism, with educational and professional studies often addressed separately through the teaching of the 'disciplines' such as sociology, psychology, philosophy and history of education (Patrick *et al.* 1982). Teaching practice came after an initial theoretical understanding and constituted an opportunity for the beginning teacher to put theory into practice. This amounted to what Pring (1996) describes as a 'theory before practice' approach to teacher education which, it was claimed, failed to address both the actual problems of professional practice and the complex professional practice of practitioners.

According to Furlong *et al.* (2000), pressure from government during the mid- to late 1980s had caused the disciplines to become noticeably absent in teacher education by 1992, and educational and professional studies were highly school-focused. As a result ITE subject specialist lecturers were responsible for the educational and professional studies of a whole group of students. By the mid- to late 1990s 'initial teacher education had become an overwhelmingly practical affair' (Furlong *et al.* 2000: 139), with students being urged to become reflective practitioners.[8] In other words, students were urged not to simply focus on practical activity but to adopt a reflective and critical stance towards it.

The concept of the 'reflective practitioner' arose from work of Schon (1983)[9] and was developed initially among university-based secondary school ITE programmes during the mid-1980s (Eraut 1994). The major theme of Schon's work was about learning by doing, of reflection-in-action, and developing a new epistemology of practice (Usher *et al.* 1997). From Schon's perspective the pedagogy of professional education should be one where the role of teacher resembles that of a coach who brings experience and research into a dialectic with the student in a situation of practice.[10] Schon focuses on how practitioners generate professional knowledge in problematic action settings. Such an approach argued that the practice of professionals does not conform to predictable technical rationality exemplified by lists of competencies or a reliable theoretical framework, because practice is unpredictable and messy, demanding a kind of intuitive understanding for which technical rationality is no preparation. In answer to the question of what makes some professionals manifestly more professional than others at dealing with uncertainty, Schon uses the word 'artistry' rather than wisdom, talent, or intuition. Inherent in the practice of professionals recognised as unusually competent is a core of 'artistry'. Students under Schon's new model should be coached rather than taught, based on the assumption that learning is done by the learner, by doing. This takes place in situations and settings that are realistic but have a low risk, with the coach guiding, advising, questioning, criticising and demonstrating, rather than teaching. The setting up and designing of learning through practice or projects is Schon's 'practicum'. Using the phrase from Polanyi (1967) of tacit knowledge – 'we can know more then we can tell' – Schon explains how the professional uses know-how and observable intelligent action without being able explain it verbally. This he calls knowing-in-action, which is different from thinking back and reflecting on past practice, which he calls reflection-on-action.

Schon's theories are concerned with explaining the complexity of professional knowledge, giving primacy to practice, and acknowledging some sort of tacit, implicit, intuitive, common-sense knowledge that is separate from other forms of knowledge because it relies on experience and knowledge gained through practice. He raises important questions and highlights the complexity of knowledge and decision making, and this is certainly useful and is often used against those who advocate narrow competencies and technical rationality.

Various writers have subsequently suggested that the concept of the 'reflective practitioner' actually serves to separate theory from practice

(Usher *et al.* 1997). Although Schon emphasises the 'artistry' of professional practice and practitioners' capacity for generating ideas and tacit knowledge, he fails to address the full implications of the self-referential nature of such 'theories in use' and such 'knowledge-in-action' (Humes 1996). Usher argues that the meaning of a 'theory-in-use' or 'knowing-in-action' is highly situated (Usher *et al.* 1997). It is dependent upon interpretations made in particular contexts and in relation to specific cultural conventions and contexts. It does not therefore readily provide concepts or criteria that allow professionals to assess and relate different 'theories-in-use' to one another or to research-based knowledge (Eraut 1994).

A fundamental criticism made of Schon is that he over-emphasises reflection on individual experience and does not take into account the view that a combination of experiences from different people can be the basis for new theoretical knowledge and understanding that could not have been achieved individually (Humes 1996). For example, what happens when professionals take different positions on the same problems, as is often the case in teaching (Young and Lucas 1999)? What then happens to the infallibility of professional judgement when in practice many positions are put, and a choice has to be made? Surely, some deliberative or rational choice may be appropriate even when choice is uncertain and contains an element of risk (Beck 1992)?

Overall, there is widespread agreement with Schon that a large part of teaching relies on professional judgement often based upon experience built up over time (Munby and Russell 1993). However, having made a professional judgement, some framework for analysing the reasons for the decision needs to be utilised outside the individual's intuitive knowledge. Professional decisions, particularly in teaching, are in the public domain and professionals have to justify their decisions and expertise, not only to the public, but also to each other if professions are to change and develop new knowledge (Eraut 1994). Tacit knowledge may be a part of what teachers know; however, as Shulman (1988) suggests, it is the obligation of teacher educators to make the tacit explicit (Evans 2002). Teachers improve when they get explicit answers from colleagues or ITE teachers. And making things explicit lies at the heart of the professional development of the teacher, which is itself a combination of reflection on practical experience and a reflection on broader experiences of others, research and theoretical understanding. In this respect concerns have been raised about the limitations of using the idea of 'reflective practice' as the basis of a model of FE professionalism because of the diversity and changing role of the FE teacher (Guile and Lucas 1999).

The FE teacher as reflective practitioner

At the same time as the concept of the 'reflective practitioner' was being adopted by teacher education departments in school-focused ITE programmes, it was also taken up by ITE programmes for the further education sector (Lucas *et al.* 1996). In FE teacher education the concept of the 'reflective practitioner' was also used as a concept upon which to base ideas about professional practice in the teacher's own understanding and experience of their working practices. Moreover, it has also been used to assist FE teachers to develop a critical approach to their professional practice. By the late 1990s the concept of the 'reflective practitioner' featured in almost all FE teacher training programmes[11] (Elliott 1998) and the concept has now been incorporated into the national standards for FE teachers being implemented by the National Training Organisation for FE colleges (FENTO 1999).

However, the model of the 'reflective practitioner' has been interpreted in many different ways in FE ITE, and remains ambiguous. It would seem that most teacher educators work to a common-sense definition of reflection which has become an appealing term, not really articulated other than to encourage teachers to be thoughtful about what they have done and what they plan to do in the future. It has also been used as a way of limiting the mechanical application of competences designed to make ITE courses similar to NVQs (Guile and Lucas 1999). This has led to some 'well intentioned developments' in ITE courses (Munby and Russell 1993) and used to encourage beginning teachers to reflect on and learn from experience to meet new situations. Concepts of reflection have also added to the critique of competence models, which are widely seen as over-mechanistic and inadequate as a basis for the training of teachers (Hyland 1994).

A major reservation concerning Schon's use of reflection is that it over-stresses professional learning as an individual teacher activity (Humes 1996), rather than seeing the professional as a member of a wider community. Importantly, the professional knowledge of FE teachers does not develop in isolation. It also develops in relation to the interaction with others in the 'community of practice' and broader systems of relationships both inside and outside the FE college (Harkin *et al.* 2001). This extended view of learning explains how a teacher can learn not only within, but also between contexts, using decontextualised knowledge or (decontextualising it) in order to apply it to other contexts. There is a danger that the model of 'reflective practitioner', uncritically applied, may lead FE teachers down a road where reflection becomes a routine 'navel gazing' matter (Huddleston and Unwin 1997) which fails to place professional practice within a broader context (Hillier 2002). Reflection is a very necessary element in a teacher's professional knowledge. However, it is by no means sufficient and by itself can only be 'partial in the absence of a reflexive critique of the situatedness of practice' (Usher *et al.* 1997: 169); 'encouraging teachers to become reflective practitioners (whatever that may mean) may be limiting them to the confines of their personal knowledge and to a private engagement to it' (Hoyle and John 1995: 76).

Conclusion

This chapter has explored four dominant models of professional practice. It began by tracing the development of standards and competencies in relation to vocational education and training qualifications in the UK, suggesting that the interpretation of competence and standards in FE colleges was different from schools because of FE's links with industrial models of training and the resulting 'training culture'. Subsequently, the concept of the FE college teacher as 'competent practitioner', although arising from vocational traditions, became a general model used to define the practices upon which all FE teachers are judged.

Concepts of the teacher as 'subject specialist' and 'reflective practitioner' were initially developed without the FE teacher in mind. Notions of the teacher as 'reflective practitioner' were developed within school initial teacher education as a reconceptualisation of the 'subject specialist'. The appeal of 'reflection' was its flexibility of meaning and interpretation, and its means of encouraging teachers to reflect upon and be critical of their own practical experiences and understandings.

While these four models do not describe all the professional practices of FE teachers, they do highlight major divisions of professional practice in the sector. Although few now suggest that subject or vocational knowledge is sufficient to teach, there is a tension highlighted between the emphasis given to subject knowledge in recent Ofsted reports and the competence/standards model reflected in sector skills councils. This tension has been highlighted by a recent NRDC (Lucas *et al.* 2004) evaluation of ITE programmes that focuses on the balance to be struck between subject knowledge and more generic pedagogic and professional issues.

Ultimately, neither the competent nor the reflective practitioner models are sufficient on their own. Both models focus upon the FE teacher's own understandings, experience and practice, perpetuating the rather narrow focus upon subject or vocational knowledge and thus reproducing the custom and practices of many subject and vocational departments (Robson 1998).

Notes

1 This refers to methods that were the fashion of the time, often consisting of programmed learning packs, with cards and indexes, etc. for students to use to learn at their own pace in learning workshops. This became most sophisticated in the teaching of foreign languages.
2 The introduction of national standards in 1999 and compulsory teacher education for all new FE teachers in 2001 is changing this culture.
3 Wolf concedes that whilst the critique of education was well founded the alternative put forward was, unfortunately, less so.
4 The TDLB units were later applied to teachers of GNVQs and the competence-based approaches to ITE and staff development were not just confined to the 'vocational specialist'.

5 On examination of the questions asked in the survey, no definition of competence was given or required; therefore 'having stated outcomes' could have been construed as being competence-based in the narrow or broad sense.

6 The focus is on secondary school teachers. Primary teachers are another case. Sometimes they are portrayed as having a more collaborative culture and practising an extended teacher professionalism (Hoyle 1974). Others describe how it is a contrived collegiality (Hargreaves 1994) where the primary teacher's practice is becoming more and more prescribed with a consequent lack of professionalism.

7 According to Ferguson and Womak (1993), in-depth knowledge of subject matter beyond the certification threshold required in the USA made little difference when measured against the quality of teaching and learning. They suggest that subject knowledge is important as a basis for teaching, but extending subject knowledge beyond the entry requirements for teaching does not increase the quality of the teaching. Candidates who had been through teacher education courses, however, tended to show an increase in teacher sensitivity with more knowledge about methods of teaching and judging their effectiveness (Everson *et al.* 1985; Skipper and Quantz 1987).

8 Furlong *et al.* (2000) also show that while the universities studied saw the 'reflective practitioner' model of teacher education as a means of criticising current practice most student teachers saw it as a pragmatic strategy for thinking through and sharing practical experience.

9 The 'reflective practitioner' was not conceived of originally for teachers in particular, but was developed mainly as a concept for teachers in schools.

10 When Schon refers to 'teacher' he is not referring to school or FE teacher, but more of a mentor in the professional workplace whom he describes as a coach or reflective supervisor (Schon 1988).

11 Often alongside the concept of the 'competent practitioner' (see chapter 4).

10 Towards a new professional framework for teachers in further education

This book has sought to explore different ways of understanding and conceptualising the professional practice of FE teachers. The argument has been offered that the practices of FE teachers are best understood by appreciating their vocational roots, the historical neglect of the sector by successive governments, and the diversity of teaching and learning found in the sector. Although this diversity of practice is not new, circumstances have changed, from a variation that arose from local initiatives and a *laissez-faire* approach from central government to a fragmentation of provision that had been exacerbated by a context of national regulation, reflecting efforts by government to raise standards and make FE more accountable.

The FE sector, as it became known during the time of the FEFC, has now been subsumed by the Learning and Skills Sector. Yet, in spite of recent reforms, it still lacks a clear identity and continues to exhibit 'strategic drift' in vision and purpose (Green and Lucas 1999a). Despite efforts to encourage co-operation, there is still competition between schools, sixth-form/tertiary and FE colleges to recruit 16–19-year-olds. FE colleges still cater for an increasingly diverse group of learners, offering an expanding range of courses including HE programmes, A levels, vocational courses, NVQs, general vocational courses, adult basic skills provision, and access courses. This book shows that even with all the recent reforms and initiatives, general FE colleges are still caught between the priorities of preparatory and lifelong learning and general and vocational education. On the one hand colleges are urged by government and government bodies to serve national skill needs and on the other hand they are encouraged to respond to other new initiatives to cater for the socially excluded, and meet local community needs (as well as to cater for the needs of 14–19-year-olds).

Throughout this book, it has been argued that there has been little research focusing on teachers in FE and ideas concerning the professional practice of FE teachers. Ideas about such practice have been drawn eclectically from sources such as the traditional links colleges have had with employment and training cultures, a wide range of different vocational and pre-vocational traditions, as well as models based on teaching in schools. The diversity of practice within FE is double-edged in its consequences; it is a strength in meeting the variety of learning needs and destinations of FE students, yet it also acts as an obstacle to FE teachers arriving at some common understanding of professional practice or engaging in wider discussions concerning teaching and learning. In chapters 8 and 9 several different ways of conceptualising the professional practice of FE teachers were explained and the conclusion was reached that no one model or teaching and learning tradition was adequate to act as an exemplar for all FE teachers.

One possible way forward may be for FE teachers to change from identifying primarily as subject or vocational specialists to identifying themselves as professional further education teachers first, and specialists second. However, as was argued in chapter 8, the diversity of professional practice amongst FE teachers is far too complex and deeply embedded to be overcome in this way. This complexity is illustrated in the difference between two seemingly contradictory but widely held views concerning the practice of teaching in general, but exemplified when applied to FE teaching. The first view sees teaching as essentially a practical, common-sense activity that is undertaken within particular specialisations. Here subject or vocational knowledge is primary, and, combined with a 'love of subject', teaching can be learned on the job. The second view argues that a large part of teaching and learning is generic and cuts across specialisations, and that common standards of professional practice should be required of teachers no matter what their subject or vocational specialisation. Policy makers swing between both positions, sometimes emphasising the importance of subject knowledge and sometimes emphasising generic standards.

As shown throughout this book, the difficulty lies in finding a balance between contradictory pressures and positions. This is exacerbated because there is no common professional culture among FE teachers that can mediate between seemingly irreconcilable positions. For example, little discussion takes place among FE teachers concerning the relationship between how something is taught and the knowledge of the person teaching it, or the balance to be found between the content of teaching and the teaching itself. In the absence of a professional culture which discusses teaching and learning, the increased regulation of FE teachers has brought to the fore the tension between different subject and vocational specialisations that has always divided teachers. All recent policy initiatives, such as the introduction of FENTO standards to improve ITE and professional development, have been taking place within a fragmented and impoverished professional culture, which has a tendency towards compliance to the latest initiative rather than engaging in and changing policy. It is this set of divided contradictory practices and views, combined with the lack of clear vision and purpose about which group of learners FE is there to serve, that sets the wider context for recent policy reforms and regulation. It is these diverse and seemingly contradictory pressures of division, diversity and regulation that are at the hub of the many challenges facing policy makers and FE teachers.

In this final chapter, three major themes emerging from the analysis offered will be discussed. First, it will be argued that the learning and skills sector is too diverse to be regulated against one set of criteria and needs realigning in order to give institutions a clearer strategic focus. Second, it is proposed that the FENTO standards and the 'occupational standards approach' should be replaced by professional standards with a framework akin to that of schoolteachers. Third, it will be suggested that existing models and discussions concerning the professional practice and attributes of FE teachers are too narrow and that a rethinking of the FE teacher as a 'learning professional' is a constructive way forward.

Realigning further education

As suggested in chapter 7, the FE sector (let alone the learning and skills sector) remains too diverse in its purposes and practices to have a clear strategic vision. In such circumstances, a common notion of standards and a clear professional identity are unachievable in any meaningful sense. It is hard to see how FE is going to strategically change under the new LSC arrangements, when no clear vision for the sector is emerging and no real strategic leadership is being given by central government. There was some implicit suggestion in government papers that arrangements for 16–19-year-olds would be separately provided, although this seems no longer the case. As was demonstrated in chapter 3, the obstacles to bringing about strategic, area-wide collaboration are formidable, particularly in the context of a fragmented planning structure and diverse institutional interests. In any case FE colleges, sixth forms in schools, tertiary colleges and other adult providers do not draw students from one LSC area. Furthermore, getting local employer involvement is very difficult and there are considerable reservations concerning the ability of employer-led bodies to carry through this difficult strategic task.

Unlike sixth-form and 16–19 tertiary colleges, general FE colleges have never had a clear strategic vision. Meanwhile, HE institutions, particularly the 'new universities', have moved decisively into the mature student market with the expansion of foundation, access and other sub-degree provision for local students. As a result general FE colleges are being squeezed by the school sector, 16–19 institutions, training providers and HE and need a clearer definition of their function and clientele, with more clearly defined boundaries.[1]

One way of achieving this clearer strategic definition might be to restructure the sector along the lines of its major divisions. This would create comprehensive 16–19 tertiary colleges, 19+ adult FE colleges, and a clear demarcation and boundary between FE and HE provision (Green and Lucas 1999a).[2] Institutions focusing on the learning needs of 16–19-year-olds could build upon the successes of sixth-form and tertiary colleges. Such institutions already outstrip schools and general FE colleges on retention and achievement for 16–19-year-olds (Kingston 2003). Tertiary colleges record higher achievement rates for their students than sixth-form colleges at all levels, and provide a much wider curriculum (RCU 2003).[3] Evidence would suggest that comprehensive tertiary colleges serve the needs of 16–19-year-olds more successfully then any other providers.

While a comprehensive 16–19 tertiary system would be politically difficult to achieve in the face of the school sixth-form provision, in the long term such a rationalisation may become possible. This could be achieved by having a clear strategic vision, providing high quality 16–19 tertiary college provision in an area which would be attractive to learners and parents, while using the new LSC 16–19 funding method as a lever for such change. This would rescue some schools from trying to maintain non-viable sixth-form provision, allowing them to concentrate on the pre-16 curriculum.

Universities could thereby become regional HE providers and regain their mission of providing degree and higher-level education. Some links could be forged between FE and universities to provide courses such as foundation degrees. However, sub-degree provision, like foundation and access courses, would be largely provided in colleges. There may need to be some regional variation, with the respective roles of the further and higher education sectors clearly demarcated, which would be good for maintaining the distinctive mission of universities.

The nearest institutional equivalent for the future of the general FE college is that of the community college in the USA. Following this pattern would mean FE colleges becoming exclusively adult institutions, devoted to adult further education and training and focusing on widening participation, social inclusion and the learning needs of the local community.

There could be problems in such a reorganisation. FE colleges that no longer cater for 16–19-year-olds could come to specialise in programmes for adult second chance learners and weaken their vocational provision as they become more diverse adult institutions. Building on the present initiatives to fund vocational centres some means could be found to help many FE colleges to restore their vocational mission and identity, which has become somewhat lost in last few decades. There is an argument for dividing adult education itself, particularly in urban areas, with some FE institutions regaining a primary vocational focus and others offering more general education programmes. This may be too radical a step. However, fewer specialist vocational FE colleges with good employer links may be able to provide significant levels of provision in particular vocational areas, and provide a robust occupational and professional culture.

Such a reorganisation would improve the provision for learners, and allow FE teachers within the different institutions to develop a common identity as teachers focused upon the specific needs of more homogeneous groups of learners.

From occupational to professional standards

As explained in chapter 7, the proposed Lifelong Learning Sector Skills Councils are to set occupational standards for the whole of the Learning and Skills Sector including HE, as well as for every other SSC as well. In some ways it seems that setting standards has become a panacea for solving the skills shortages of the UK. With such a strategy in mind, is it just a matter of redefining and reworking some of the FENTO standards as has been suggested by the DfES, so they can be universally applied across the learning and skills sector? The theory is that once the standards are mapped against existing provision to prove 'coverage' they will become applicable to all the diverse contexts in which teaching and learning take place. Such an approach takes little notice of the sector's diverse cultures, traditions and divisions and, consequently, the application of the FENTO standards becomes a farcical, paper-based exercise that does not include lesson observation or asking the opinion of learners. In such circumstances gaining endorsement is a matter of complying with a regulatory body by producing 'paper evidence' with very little changing in the delivery of ITE programmes. Furthermore, the FENTO standards are, like all occupational standards or competencies, open to wide interpretation both in terms of what they really mean and the level at which they should be applied, reflecting the problem that there are no standards for applying the standards.

In the face of the recent criticism FENTO standards have received from OFSTED and others, it is worth asking whether the 'occupational standards approach' is an appropriate way to ensure the quality of the professional practice of FE teachers. Occupational standards attempt to specify in detail what teachers do in the diverse settings of the learning and skills sector. The analysis of this book would suggest that detailed standards cannot be applied to such diverse learner needs and learning contexts. Rather than using 'occupational standards', a more worthwhile course would be to adopt a set of professional standards that defines a general framework for thinking about what FE teachers do. The lack of a general framework potentially incapacitates FE teachers not only in relation to the practical aspects of their work, but also in relation to its professional aspects (Squires 1999). While teachers need expertise in teaching that involves routine skills, they also need a general framework about the nature of their work, the professional values of being an FE teacher and the main theories of learning, motivation, and group processes. In other words, applying a set of national standards is no substitute for providing a professional framework for thinking and reflecting upon what FE teachers do.

A professional framework for FE teachers could provide a 'core' that could require other standards to apply to the diverse contexts that make up the learning and skill sector. One example of a more professional approach can be found in the TTA 'Standards for the Award of Qualified Teacher Status'. Although these TTA standards have their faults, they are not used in the same way as FENTO. For example, there is no attempt to specify in detail what teachers are expected to do. The TTA standards provide a framework or 'common understanding' that stresses the importance of professional judgement made at different times and in different contexts. This is a long way from the FENTO standards, which are based upon notions of competence where ITE courses have to map their provision against hundreds of specifications. It is important to stress the distinction between occupational and professional standards because both have quite different origins and both carry quite different meanings. The choice facing FE teachers is whether to follow the industrial, occupational standards route or have a professional framework and a professional body, akin to that of schoolteachers.

Rethinking the professional role of FE teachers

The challenge facing FE and its teachers is multi-dimensional. However, as this book has shown, the FE sector offers a much more diverse set of education and training programmes to a broader range of learners than any other education sector, yet very little research or rethinking has been done concerning the professional role of its teachers. The result has been a rather partial view of the process of teaching and teachers' perceptions of the wider professional dimensions of their role. Perhaps the first task of a professional body for FE should be to re-examine the role of the FE teacher, taking into account changes in work, society, learning and technology (Young 1998).

From earlier research, it has been suggested that pressures on FE teachers could be conceptualised in terms of a series of shifts away from traditional 'insular' notions of professional knowledge that focused on delivering subject and vocational specialism (Young *et al.* 1995). In practice, there has been increasing pressure for FE teachers to show how their specialism relates to other vocational or subject specialisms, including other areas of the curriculum and generic skills. This change has been described as a shift from subject to curriculum knowledge. As part of this shift teachers are helping learners to gain wider expertise that requires developing expertise in assignment design, small group work, counselling and tutorial skills, and the use of IT and other resource-based learning facilities. All of these changes mean FE teachers have increasingly had to become 'managers of learning', reflecting a shift away from a narrow focus on teaching to one of student learning, with the line between pedagogy and a wider professionalism becoming increasingly blurred.

In other words, FE teachers have increasingly been required to have more than a narrow knowledge about delivering a specialism in a classroom (important though that is). They have had to learn to work in multi-specialist teams requiring collaborative skills and a sufficient knowledge of the college as an organisation to enable them to link their work with other local providers such schools and training partners, thus taking account of different ways of learning and learning that takes place beyond college. Taken in combination, these changes suggest that existing ideas about the FE teacher's professional knowledge base and the conception of professional practice that underpins it has to be re-thought.

Moving beyond the notion of reflective practitioner predominately associated with schoolteachers and the training tradition allied to idea of the competent practitioner model requires a new concept. The 'learning professional' has been suggested as an alternative (Guile and Lucas 1999), because it offers a distinctive way of embracing some of the changes in the knowledge base of FE teachers. The concept of the FE teacher as a 'learning professional' denotes the need for an active engagement with the diverse needs of adult learners and the economic, educational and technological changes which have brought about new roles for FE teachers and is altering the context of all professional activity.

The concept of the 'learning professional' also draws attention to the need for a more expanded definition of the forms of specialisation and expertise than are normally associated with teaching in FE, and an extended notion of professionalism. This involves a shift from a 'curriculum-led' to a 'learner-led' perspective, with teachers as well as students becoming lifelong learners. Such an approach questions individualistic theories of learning, promotes the idea of different types of pedagogy, and suggests that learning should also be understood as a social process that takes place in 'communities of practice' (Lave and Wenger 1994).

The model of the 'learning professional' can draw and learn from school or training-based models of professional practice, while at the same time articulating the view that the role of the FE teacher is somewhat different. Such a rethinking will lead to FE teachers becoming involved in a debate about their professional role and the particular learning needs of their students. This is important, because at the end of the day, it is FE teachers themselves, in collaboration with users and policy makers, who need to set and raise their own professional standards.

Notes

1 This argument was made before the learning and skills sector was formed (Green and Lucas 1999a).
2 In some more rural areas this may not be appropriate because of distances between providers. However such circumstances would apply only to a relatively small number of learners.
3 Research has shown that, on average, tertiary colleges offered 325 qualifications and sixth-form colleges offered on average less than half that amount. The tertiary college offer included vocational, entry and academic courses. FE colleges offered 338 qualifications against the 325 of tertiary colleges, but their rates of retention and achievement were much lower than both tertiary and sixth-form colleges.

Bibliography

ACSETT (1978) *The Training of Adult and Part-time Further Education Teachers*: *Report of the Advisory Committee on the Supply and Training of Teachers* (Haycocks 2). London: DES.

— (1978a) *Training Teachers for Education Management in Further and Adult Education*: *Report of the Advisory Committee on the Supply and Training of Teachers* (Haycocks 3). London: ACSETT.

AfC (1996) *FE Now!* 24, February.

Ainley, P. (1988) *From School to YTS: Education and training in England and Wales 1944–1987*. Milton Keynes: Open University Press.

— (1990) *Vocational Education and Training*. London: Cassell.

— (1993) *Class and Skill: Changing divisions of knowledge and labour*. London: Cassell.

Ainley, P. and Bailey, B. (1997) *The Business of Learning: Staff and student experiences of further education in the 1990s*. London: Cassell.

Ainley, P. and Corney, M. (1990) *Training for the Future: The rise and fall of the Manpower Services Commission*. London: Cassell.

Ainley, P. and Rainbird, H. (eds) (1999) *Apprenticeship: Towards a new paradigm of learning*. London: Kogan Page.

Aldrich, R. (1999) 'The apprentice in history'. In A. Ainley and H. Rainbird (eds), *Apprenticeship: Towards a new paradigm of learning*. London: Kogan Page.

AoC (1999) *A National Survey of Current Practice: Assistant lecturers, instructors, supervisors and associated posts*. Circular 21/99, 7 June. London: Association of Colleges.

Argles, M. (1964) *South Kensington to Robbins: An account of English technical education and scientific education since 1851*. London: Longman.

Armitage, A., Bryant, R., Dunnill, R., Hayse, D., Hudson, A., Kent, J., Lawes, S. and Renwick, M. (2003) *Teaching and Training in Post-Compulsory Education*. Maidenhead: Open University Press.

Ashworth, P. (1993) 'Being competent and having competencies'. *Journal of Further and Higher Education* 16, 3, 8–17.

Atkinson, D. (1995) *The Dan Quayle Guide to FEFC Recurrent Funding*. Bristol: Coombe Lodge Report.

Audit Commission (1985) *Obtaining Better Value from Further Education*. London: HMSO.

Audit Commission/Ofsted (1993) *Unfinished Business: Full-time educational courses for 16-19 year olds*. London: HMSO.

Avis, J. (1987) *Curriculum Innovation in FE: A case study*. Occasional Paper. Birmingham: Centre for Contemporary Cultural Studies, University of Birmingham.

— (1990) 'Student responses to the curriculum: towards an alternative practice'. In D. Gleeson (ed.), *Training and its Alternatives*. Milton Keynes: Open University Press.

— (1999) 'Shifting identities: new conditions and the transformation of practice-teaching within post-compulsory education'. *Journal of Vocational Education and Training* 51, 2, 245–64.

Avis, J., Bathmaker, A. and Parsons, J. (2001) 'Reflections from a time-log diary: towards an analysis of the labour process within further education'. *Journal of Vocational Education and Training* 53, 1, 61–78.

Bailey, B. (1990) 'Technical education and secondary schooling, 1905–1945'. In P. Summerfield and E. Evans (eds), *Technical Education and the State since 1950*. Manchester: Manchester University Press.

— (1997) 'A historical perspective'. In G. Stanton and W. Richardson (eds), *Qualifications for the Future: A study of tripartite and other divisions in post-16 education and training*. London: FEDA.

Ball, D. and McDiarmid, G. (1990) 'The subject-matter preparation of teachers'. In R. Houstan (ed.), *Handbook of Research in Teacher Education*. New York: Macmillan.

Barnett, C. (1986) *The Audit of War: The illusion and reality of Britain as a great nation*. London: Macmillan.

Barnett, R. (1994) *The Limits of Competence*. Buckingham: SRHE/Open University Press.

Bates, A. (1995) *Technology, Open Learning and Distance Learning*. London: Routledge.

Bates, I., Clark, J., Cohen, P., Finn, D., Moore, R. and Willis, P. (1984) *Schooling for the Dole: The new vocationalism*. London: Macmillan.

Bathmaker, A. (1999) 'Managing messes and coping with uncertainty: reviewing training for teachers in post compulsory education and training'. *Journal of Further and Higher Education* 23, 2, 185–95.

Beaumont, G. (1995) *Review of 100 NVQs and SVQs*. Chesterfield: DfEE.

Beck, U. (1992) *The Risk Society*. London: Sage.

Bell, M. (1996) '7000 jobs lost'. *FE Now!* 30, 4.

Bernstein, B. (2000) *Pedagogy, Symbolic Control and Identity: Theory, research and critique*. London: Taylor and Francis.

Betts, D. (1999) 'Functional analysis of part-time staff – their roles and characteristics'. Unpublished FENTO research project. 10 November.

Bewick, T. (2003) 'We need leaders to transform skills'. *TES* (*FE Focus*) 7 November, 4.

Birch, D., Luther, J. and Spencer, A. (1987) 'Joint efficiency study of NAFE: Non teacher costs'. *Coombe Lodge Report* 19, 12. Blagdon: FE Staff College.

Birch, D., Luther, J. and Spencer, A. (1990) 'Financial Delegation for Further Education Colleges'. *Coombe Lodge Report* 21, 8. Blagdon: FE Staff College.

Bishop, A.S. (1971) *The Rise of a Central Authority in English Education*. Cambridge: Cambridge University Press.

Blackstone, T. (1998) 'Go boldly into new age of learning' *TES* (*FE Focus*) 27 March.

Bloomer, M. (1997) *Curriculum Making in Post-16 Education*. London: Routledge.

Bolton, E. (1994) 'Traditions in initial teacher training: an overview'. In M. Wilkins and D. Sankey (eds), *Collaboration and Transition in Initial Teacher Training*. London: Kogan Page.

Bradley, D. (1996) 'Who dares wins: intended and unintended consequences of the FEFC funding methodology'. *Educational Management and Administration* 24, 379–88.

— (2000) 'Cinderella FE – you shall go to the ball!' In D. Gray and C. Griffin (eds), *Post-Compulsory Education and the New Millennium*. London: Jessica Kingsley.

Bradley, J., Dee, L. and Wilenius, F. (1994) *Students with Disabilities and/or Learning Difficulties in Further Education*. Slough: NFER.

Bratchell, D.F. (1968) *The Aims and Organisation of Further Education*. Bath: Pergamon.

Bristow, A. (1970) *Inside Colleges of Further Education*. London: DES/HMSO.

Brookfield, S. (1986) *Understanding and Facilitating Adult Learning*. San Francisco: Jossey Bass.

Brooks, B. (2001) Oral report given by Barry Brooks at the DfES Initiatives on Adult Basic Skills Teaching-Steering Group. Monday 12 November. Unpublished. Caxton House: DfES.

Brooks, J. and Lucas, N. (2004) 'The changing sixth form curriculum: challenges for new teachers'. In S. Capel, M. Leask and T. Turner (eds), *Beginning to Teach in a Secondary School*. London: Routledge.

Bromley, R., Hayton, A., Mitchell, P., Lucas, N. and Young, M. (1999) *Hounslow Post 16 Progression Report*. For Hounslow LEA. London: Post 16 Education Centre, Institute of Education, University of London, March.

Burke, J. (1994) 'Theoretical issues in relation to Jessup's outcomes model'. In J. Burke (ed.), *Outcomes Learning and the Curriculum*. London: Falmer.

CACE (1959) *15–18 Crowther Report*. Central Advisory Council for England and Wales. London: HMSO.

Callaghan, Rt. Hon. J. (1976) 'Ruskin College Speech'. *Times Educational Supplement* 22 October.

Campbell, M. (2003) 'Smart moves: the skills gap'. *Guardian (Further)* 2 December, 18.

Cantor, L. and Roberts, I. (1986) *Further Education Colleges Today: A critical review* (3rd edition). London: Routledge and Kegan Paul.

Cantor, L., Roberts, I. and Prately, B. (1995) *A Guide to Further Education in England and Wales*. London: Cassell.

Capey, J. (1995) *GNVQ Assessment Review*. London: NCVQ.

Carlton, D., Gent, W. and Scammells, B. (1971) *The Administration of Technical Colleges*. Manchester: Manchester University Press.

Carlton, E. and Nash, I. (1999) 'Driving lessons offer accelerates unease'. *TES (FE Focus)*. 6 March.

Cavanagh, D. and Lancaster, D. (1983) 'Some aspects of power and its acquisition in FE colleges'. *Journal of Further and Higher Education* 7, 3, 24–36.

CBI (1989) *Towards a Skills Revolution*. London: Confederation of British Industry.

— (1994) *Quality Assessed: The CBI review of NVQs and SNVQs*. London: Confederation of British Industry.

Chambers, R. (1995) *Lewisham not Lewis! Profligate colleges or penalised students*. Praxis Papers 1. London: Lewisham College.

Chown, A. (1992) 'TDLB Standards in FE'. *Journal of Further and Higher Education* 16, 3, 52–9.

Chown, A. and Last, J. (1993) 'Can the NCVQ model be used for teacher training?' *Journal of Further and Higher Education* 17, 2, 15–25.

Clark, C. (2002) Speech to the Association of Colleges Annual Conference. Birmingham, 19 November.

Clark, L. (1999) 'The changing structure and significance of apprenticeship with special reference to construction'. In P. Ainley and H. Rainbow (eds), *Apprenticeship: Towards a new paradigm of learning*. London: Kogan Page.

Coffield, F. (1992) 'Training and Enterprise Councils: the last throw of voluntarism?' *Policy Studies* 23, 4, 11–32.

Conford, P. (1999) 'Drowned by paper in the theatre of the absurd'. *TES (FE*

Forum). 21 May, 40.

Corbett, J. and Norwich, B. (1999) 'Learners with special educational needs'. In P. Mortimore (ed.), *Understanding Pedagogy and its Impact on Learning*. London: Sage.

Cotgrove, S. (1958) *Technical Education and Social Change*. London: Allan and Unwin.

Crequer, N. (1998) 'Colleges hit the jackpot'. *TES* (*FE Focus*), 17 July.

— (1999) 'Fraud squad hit Bilston'. *TES* (*FE Focus*), 7 May.

Cripps, S. (2002) *Further Education, Government's Discourse Policy and Practice: Killing a paradigm softly*. Aldershot: Ashgate.

Dale, R. (1985) *Education, Training and Employment: Towards a new vocationalism*. Oxford: Pergamon.

Davis, B. (1997) Speech given by Brian Davis MP, Labour Party Spokesperson for FE at AoC conference, October 1997. London: Labour Party.

Davis, M. (1990) 'Technology, institutions and status: technological education, debate and policy'. In P. Summerfield and E. Evans (eds), *Technical Education and the State Since 1850*. Manchester: Manchester University Press.

Dawn, T. (1995) *Fifty Years of Further Education – Celebration or Wake?* Occasional Paper 5. Oxford: Oxford Brookes University.

Day, C. (1987) *Education and the Industrial World: The Ecole d'Arts et Métiers and the rise of French Industrial Engineering*. Cambridge, MA: MIT Press.

DE (1981) *A New Training Initiative: A programme for action*. London: HMSO.

DE/DES (1986) *Working Together: Education and training*. London: HMSO.

Dearing, R. (1996) *Review of Qualifications for 16–19 Year Olds*. London: SCAA.

Debling, G. (1989) 'The Employment Department/Training Agency Standards Programme and NVQs. Implications for education'. In J. Burke (ed.), *Competency Based Education and Training*. London: Falmer.

Dee, L. (1999) 'Inclusive learning: from rhetoric to reality'. In A. Green and N. Lucas (eds), *FE and Lifelong Learning: Realigning the sector for the 21st century*. London: Institute of Education, University of London.

Derrick, J. (1997) *Adult Part-time Learners in Colleges and the FEFC*. Post 16 Education Centre Working Paper 21. London: Institute of Education, University of London.

DES (1972) *Teacher Education and Training* (James Report). London: HMSO.

— (1972a) *Education: A Framework for Expansion*. Cmnd 5174. London: Department of Education and Science.

— (1975) *The Training of Teachers for Further Education. Report of the Advisory Committee on the Supply and Training of Teachers* (Haycocks 1). London: DES.

— (1976) 'Statistics of Education'. *Further Education*, vol. 3. London: HMSO.
— (1977) *The Training of Teachers in Further Education. Circular 11/77*. London: Department of Education and Science.
— (1979) *The Macfarlane Report. Education and Training for 16–18 year olds, a Consultative Paper*. London: HMSO.
— (1985) *Managing Colleges Efficiently*. London: HMSO.
— (1991) *Training for Teaching in Further and Adult Education: A report by HMI*. London: Department for Education and Science (ref. 19/91/NS).
DES/ED (1991) *Education and Training for the 21st Century* (vols 1 and 2). London: HMSO.
Dewey, J. (1938) 'The relation of theory to practice in education'. In R. Archambault (ed.), *John Dewey on Education*. Chicago: University of Chicago Press, 313–38.
— (1966) *Democracy and Education*. New York: Free Press.
DfEE (1995a) *NCVQ 1995 Quinquennial Review*. Stage One Report. London: DfEE.
— (1996) *Funding 16–19 Education and Training: Towards convergence*. London: Department for Education and Employment.
— (1997) *Qualifying for Success*: *A consultation paper on the future of post 16 education*. Green Paper. London: Stationery Office.
— (1998) *The Learning Age: A Renaissance for a New Britain*. London: Stationery Office.
— (1998a) *National Training Organisations: Prospectus 1998–99*. Sudbury: Department of Education and Employment.
— (1999) *National Training Organisations: Prospectus 1999–2000*. Sudbury: Department of Education and Employment.
— (1999a) 'Paper produced for DfEE Colloquium'. Unpublished paper. Birmingham: June.
— (1999b) *Learning to Succeed: A new framework for post 16 learning*. White Paper. London: Stationery Office.
— (2000) *Learning to Succeed. Post 16 Funding and Allocations: First technical consultation paper*. London: DfEE, January.
— (2000a) *Consultation Paper on the Introduction of Compulsory Teaching Qualifications for FE College Teachers*. London: DfEE.
DfEE/FEDA (1995) *Mapping the FE Sector*. Peterborough: FEDA.
— DfES (2002) *Success For All: Reforming further education and training. Discussion document – June 2002*. Online. Available HTTP:<http://www.dfes.gov.uk/learningandskills/pdf/SuccessForAll.pdf> (accessed 28 April 2004).
— (2002a) *Delivering Skills for Life: Skills for life*. Nottingham: Department for

Education and Skills.

— (2002b) *Success for All: Reforming further education and training. Our vision for the future – November 2002.* Online. Available HTTP:<http://www.teachernet.gov.uk/_doc/4760/sucessforallr[1].pdf> (accessed 28 April 2004).

— (2003) *The Future of Initial Teacher Education for the Learning and Skills Sector.* London: Department of Education and Skills/Standards Unit.

DfES/FENTO (2002) *Subject Specifications for Teachers of Adult Literacy and Numeracy.* London: FENTO.

Donovan Commission (1968) *Report of the Royal Commission on Trade Unions and Employers' Associations.* London: HMSO.

Drodge, S. and Cooper, N. (1997) 'The Management and Strategic Planning in FE Colleges'. In R. Levacic and R. Glatter (eds), *Managing Change in Further Education.* FEDA Report 1 (7). London: FEDA.

Dyson, A. and Millward, A. (1997) 'The reform of special education or the transformation of mainstream schools'. In S. Meijer, D. Pijl and S. Hegerty (eds), *Inclusive Education: A global agenda.* London: Routledge.

Ecclestone, K. (1995) *Can NVQs be a Framework for Academic Staff Development?'* Briefing Paper 22. Sheffield: University and Colleges Staff Development Agency.

— (1997) 'Energising or enervating: implications of NVQs in professional development'. *Journal of Vocational Education and Training* 49, 1, 65–79.

— (2000) 'Bewitched, bothered and bewildered: a policy analysis of the GNVQ assessment regime 1992–2000'. *Journal of Education Policy* 15, 5, 532–58.

— (2002) *Learning Autonomy in Post-16 Education: The politics and practice of formative assessment.* London: RoutledgeFalmer.

Edam, A., Spencer, P. and Fyfield, B. (2003) *Organisation of Provision of Post 16 Training: A report to the DfES to inform the design of guidance on the conduct of Strategic Area Reviews.* London: Learning and Skills Development Agency.

ED/DES (1986) *Working Together – Education and Training.* London: HMSO.

Education and Employment Committee (1998) *Sixth Report of the House of Commons Education and Employment Committee.* Vols 1 and 2 (Hodge Report). 19 May. London: Stationery Office.

Edwards, H. (1961) *The Evening Institute: Its place in the educational system in England and Wales.* London: National Institute of Adult Education.

Edwards, T. (1997) 'Educating leaders and training followers'. In T. Edwards, C. Fitz-Gibbon, F. Hardman, R. Haywood and N. Meagher (eds), *Separate But*

Equal? A Levels and GNVQS. London: Routledge.

Edwards, T., Fitz-Gibbon, C., Hardman, F., Haywood, R. and Meagher, N. (1997) *Separate But Equal? A Levels and GNVQS*. London: Routledge.

Elliott, G. (1997) 'Learning and teaching in post-compulsory education: a lifetime perspective'. *Research in Post-Compulsory Education* 2, 3, 249–59.

— (2000) 'The management of teaching in further education: issues from a case study'. In D. Gray and C. Griffin (eds), *Post-Compulsory Education and the New Millennium*. London: Jessica Kingsley.

Elliott, G. and Hall, V. (1994) 'FE Inc – business orientation in FE and the introduction of human resource management'. *School Organisation* 14, 1, 3–10.

Elliott, J. (1993) *Reconstructing Teacher Education*. London: Falmer.

— (1998) 'Lecturing in post-compulsory education: profession, occupation or reflective practice? *Teachers and Teaching: Theory and Practice* 4, 1, 161–74.

ELS (1996) *Education Lecturing Resource Pack*. Leeds: Education Lecturing Service.

Elsdon, K. (1975) *Training for Adult Education*. Nottingham: University of Nottingham, Department of Adult Education.

Eraut, M. (1994) *Developing Professional Knowledge and Competence*. London: Falmer.

Esland, G. (1996) 'Education and training and nation state capitalism: Britain's failing strategy'. In R. Edwards, A. Hanson and P. Raggatt (eds), *Boundaries of Adult Learning*. Milton Keynes: Open University Press.

Evans, B. (1987) *Radical Adult Education: A political critique*. London: Croom Helm.

Evans, K. (1975) *The Development and Structure of the English Education System*. Sevenoaks: Hodder and Stoughton.

Evans, K. (2002) 'The Challenges of "making learning visible": problems and issues in recognising tacit skills and key competences'. In K. Evans, P. Hodkinson and L. Unwin (eds), *Working to Learn: Transforming learning in the workplace*. London: Kogan Page.

Everson, C., Hawley, W. and Zlotniik, M. (1985) 'Making a difference in educational quality through teacher education'. *Journal of Teacher Education* 36, 2, 2–10.

Farnham, D. and Horton, S. (1993) *Managing the New Public Services*. Basingstoke: Macmillan.

Fawbett, F. (2003) *Teaching in Post-Compulsory Education: Learning, skills and standards*. London: Continuum.

FEDA (1999) 'FENTO qualifications and recognition framework'. Paper presented to expert seminar, Vauxhall. 26 July.

— (1999a) 'FENTO qualifications and recognition framework'. Paper presented to expert seminar, Vauxhall. October.

— (1999b) 'FENTO qualifications and recognition framework'. Further paper presented to expert seminar, Vauxhall. October.

FEFC (1992) *Funding Learning*. Coventry: Further Education Funding Council.

— (1992a) *Preparing for Incorporation*. Coventry: Further Education Funding Council.

— (1993) *Further Consultation on Funding Learning*. London: Further Education Funding Council.

— (1996) *Quality and Standards in Further Education Colleges in England*. Chief Inspector's Report 1995/96. Coventry: Further Education Funding Council.

— (1996a) *Teaching and Learning with Information and Learning Technology*. Coventry: Further Education Funding Council.

— (1996b) *Inclusive Learning: Report of the Learning Difficulties and/or Disabilities Committee*. London: HMSO.

— (1998) *Funding Guidance 1999/2000. Circ 99/07*. Coventry: Further Education Funding Council.

— (1999) *Funding Tariff for 99–2000. Circ 99/01*. Coventry: Further Education Funding Council.

— (1999a) *Consultations on the Recommendations of the Widening Participation Committee. Circ 98/07*. Coventry: Further Education Funding Council.

— (1999b) *Professional Development in Further Education. National Report from the FEFC Inspectorate*. Coventry: Further Education Funding Council.

FE Now! (1997) 'My kind of town'. *FE Now!* 36, April, 9.

FENTO (1999) *National Standards for Teaching and Supporting Learning in Further Education in England and Wales*. London: FENTO.

— (2000) *National Occupational Standards for Management in Further Education*. Draft 6, 1 February. London: FENTO.

— (2002) 'English National Advisory Committee. Report by the Director of Quality and Standards'. Unpublished report. 24 September.

Ferguson, P. and Womack, S. (1993) 'The impact of subject matter and education coursework on teacher performance'. *Journal of Teacher Education* 44, 1, 55–63.

Ferguson, R. and Abbott, A. (1935) *Day Continuation Schools*. London: Pitman.

FESDF (1997) 'Standards Sub Group Report'. S97/02B Further Education Staff Development Forum. Unpublished report. 8 April.

— (1997a) 'Awarding Body Sub-Group'. Further Education Staff Development Forum. Unpublished report. 10 April.

— (1997b) 'Notes from the inaugural meeting of the Awarding Bodies Sub-Group'. Unpublished report. London: FEDA. 20 January.

FEU (1989) *Towards an Educational Audit*. London: FEU.

— (1992) *Consultation on Qualifications Based on TDLB Standards* (RP717). London: Further Education Unit.

— (1994) 'FEU HE Providers Seminar'. Unpublished minutes. 14 October.

— (1994a) 'HE Cert. ED (FE) Providers Seminar' (TDLB). Unpublished notes of meeting at the FEU on 17 December.

Finegold, D. and Soskice, D. (1988) 'The failure of training in Britain: analysis and prescription'. *Oxford Review of Economic Policy* 4, 3, 232–51.

Foden, F. (1992) *The Education of Part-Time Teachers in Further and Adult Education*. London: Further Education Unit.

Forum (1997) *Standards Development and Learning Support in FE*. Forum Workshop Papers. 21 October.

Frankel, A. and Reeves, F. (1996) *The Further Education Curriculum in England: An introduction*. Bilston: Bilston College Publications.

Freire, P. (1970) *Pedagogy of the Oppressed* (trans. M. Ramer). Harmondsworth: Penguin.

Fryer Report (1997) *Learning for the 21st Century*. First Report. London: NAGCELL.

Fuller, A. and Unwin, L. (1998) 'Reconceptualising apprenticeship: exploring the relationship between work and learning'. *Journal of Vocational Education and Training* 50, 2, 12–20.

Fuller, A. and Unwin, L. (2002) 'Developing pedagogies for the contemporary workplace.' In K. Evans, P. Hodkinson and L. Unwin (eds), *Working to Learn: Transforming learning in the workplace*. London: Kogan Page.

Furlong, J., Barton, L., Miles, S., Whiting, C. and Whitty, G. (2000) *Teacher Education in Transition: Reforming professionalism*. Buckingham: Open University Press.

Garland, P. (1993) 'Competence based qualifications for FE lecturers'. *Journal of Further and Higher Education* 17, 2, 86–9.

Gee, R. (1997) 'Introduction'. In R. Levacic and R. Glatter (eds), *Managing Change in Further Education*. FEDA Report 1 (7). London: FEDA.

Gleeson, D. (1990) 'Skills training and its alternatives'. In D. Gleeson (ed.), *Training and its Alternatives*. Milton Keynes: Open University Press.

— (1996) 'Post-compulsory education in a post-industrial and post-modern age'. In J. Avis, M. Bloomer, G. Esland and P. Hodgkinson (eds), *Knowledge and Nationhood*. London: Cassell.

— (2001) 'Style and substance in education leadership: further education as a case in point'. *Journal of Education Policy* 16, 3, 181–96.

Gleeson, D. and Mardle, G. (1980) *Further Education or Training?* London: Routledge and Kegan Paul.

Gleeson, D. and Shain, F. (1999) 'Managing ambiguity: between markets and managerialism – a case study of middle managers in further education'. *The Sociological Review* 47, 3, 461–90.

Gleeson, D. and Smith, G. (1987) '16–18 the neglected territory of TVEI provision'. In D. Gleeson (ed.), *TVEI and the Secondary School: A critical appraisal*. Milton Keynes: Open University Press.

Gorringe, R. (1996) *Changing the Culture of a College*. Coombe Lodge Report 24, 3. Bristol: The Staff College.

Gravatt, J. (2001) Unpublished paper produced for staff and governor training. London: City Lit.

Graham, I. (1997) 'Principals' responses to incorporation and the new funding regime'. *Journal of Vocational Education and Training* 49, 4, 545–62.

Green, A. (1997) *Education, Globalization and the Nation State*. London: Macmillan.

Green, A. and Lucas, N. (1999) 'From obscurity to crisis: the FE sector in context'. In A. Green and N. Lucas (eds), *FE and Lifelong Learning: Realigning the sector for the 21st century*. London: Institute of London, University of London.

Green, A. and Lucas, N. (1999a) 'Repositioning further education: a sector for the twenty-first century'. In A. Green and N. Lucas (eds), *FE and Lifelong Learning: Realigning the sector for the 21st century*. London: Institute of Education, University of London.

Guile, D. and Hayton, A. (1999) 'Information and learning technology: the implications for teaching and learning in further education'. In A. Green and N. Lucas (eds), *FE and Lifelong Learning: Realigning the sector for the 21st century*. London: Institute of Education, University of London.

Guile, D. and Lucas, N. (1996) 'Preparing for the future: the training and professional development of staff in the FE sector'. *Journal of Teacher Development* 5, 3, 47–55.

Guile, D. and Lucas, N. (1999) 'Rethinking initial teacher education and professional development in FE: towards the learning professional'. In A. Green and N. Lucas (eds), *FE and Lifelong Learning: Realigning the sector for the 21st century*. London: Institute of Education, University of London.

Hall, J. (2000) 'PGCE (FE) training salaries for 2000–2001'. Unpublished letter from DfEE FE Standards Team to UCET.

Hall, V. (1994) *Further Education in the United Kingdom* (2nd edition). Bristol: Collins Educational and Coombe Lodge.

Handy, C. (1989) *The Age of Unreason*. London: Arrow Books.

Hargreaves, A. (1994) *Changing Teachers, Changing Times: Teachers Work and Culture in a Post Modern Age*. London: Cassell.

Harkin, J. (1995) 'The impact of GNVQs on the communication styles of teachers'. Paper for UCET Conference, October. Oxford: School of Education, Oxford Brookes University.

— (1998) 'Constructs used by vocational students in England to evaluate their teachers'. *Journal of Vocational Education and Training* 50, 3, 339–53.

Harkin, J., Turner, G. and Dawn, T. (2001) *Teaching Young Adults: A handbook for teachers in post-compulsory education*. London: RoutledgeFalmer.

Harkin, J., Clow, R. and Hillier, Y. (2003) *Recollected in Tranquillity? FE teachers' perceptions of their initial teacher training*. London; Learning and Skills Development Agency.

Harper, D. (2000) 'New college hierarchies: towards an examination of organisational structures in FE in England and Wales'. *Educational Management and Administration* 28, 4, 433–45.

Harrison, J. (1954) *History of the Working Men's College 1854–1954*. London: Routledge and Kegan Paul.

Hill, R. (2000) 'A study of full-time further education lecturers regarding their colleges' corporations and agencies of the further education sector'. *Journal of Further and Higher Education* 24, 1, 67–77.

Hillier, Y. (2002) *Reflective Teaching in Further and Adult Education*. London: Continuum.

HMI (1983) *Teaching in Schools: The content of initial teacher training*. London: DES.

— (1991) *The TVEI in England and Wales*. London: HMI/DES.

— (2004) 'Consultation on the Ofsted "Framework for the inspection of the initial training of further education teachers"'. HMI 2202, March 2004. London: Ofsted.

Hoare, S. and Kingston, P. (2003) 'Conflicts of Interest'. *Guardian Education (Further)* 9 September, 58.

Hodgson, A. and Spours, K. (1997) *Dearing and Beyond: 14–19 qualifications, frameworks and systems*. London: Kogan Page.

Hodgson, A. and Spours, K. (1999) *New Labour's Educational Agenda: Issues and policies for education and training from 14+*. London: Kogan Page.

Hodgson, A. and Spours, K. (2003) *Beyond A Levels: Curriculum 2000 and the reform of 14–19 qualifications*. London: Kogan Page.

Hodkinson, P. (1992) 'Alternative models of competence in vocational education and training'. *Journal of Further and Higher Education* 16, 2, 30–9.

— (1995) 'Professionalism and competence'. In P. Hodkinson and M. Issitt (eds), *The Challenge of Competence*. London: Cassell.

Hodkinson, P. (1998) 'Technicism, teachers and teaching quality in vocational education and training'. *Journal of Vocational Education and Training* 50, 2,

193–208.

Holloway, D. (1999) 'The Audit Commission, managerialism and the further education sector'. *Journal of Vocational Education and Training* 51, 2, 229–44.

Hook, S. (2003) 'Seats on shadow board agreed'. *THES (FE Focus)* 10 October, 1.

Hoyle, E. (1974) 'Professionality, professionalism and control in teacher education. *London Educational Review* 3, 2, 13–19.

Hoyle, E. and John, P. (1995) *Professional Knowledge and Professional Practice*. London: Cassell.

Huddlestone, P. and Unwin, L. (1997) *Teaching and Learning in Further Education: Diversity and change*. London: Routledge.

Humes, W. (1996) 'Towards a new agenda for teacher education'. Paper given at the Association for Teacher Education in Europe Conference in Glasgow, 1–6 September, 1–22.

Hughs, C. (2002) Unpublished speech delivered to FE governors, NATFHE.

Hyland, T. (1994) *Competence Education and NVQs*. London: Cassell.

— (1995) 'Behaviourism and the meaning of competence'. In P. Hodkinson and M. Issitt (eds), *The Challenge of Competence*. London: Cassell.

Hyland, T. and Merrill, B. (2003) *The Changing Face of Further Education: Lifelong learning, inclusion and community values in further education*. London: RoutledgeFalmer.

Ifl (2003) Institute for Teaching (PCET) website: www.ifl.ac.uk.

Illich, I. (1973) *Deschooling Society*. Harmondsworth: Penguin.

James Report (1972) *Teacher Education and Training*. London: HMSO.

Jarvis, P. (1983) *Professional Education*. London: Croom Helm.

— (1995) *Adult and Continuing Education: Theory and Practice*. London: Routledge.

Jessup, G. (1991) *Outcomes: NVQs and the emerging model of education and training*. London: Falmer.

Jones, L. and Mooore, R. (1993) 'Education, competence and the control of expertise'. *British Journal of Education* 14, 4, 385–97.

Kennedy, H. (1997) *Learning Works: Widening participation in further education colleges*. Coventry: FEFC.

Kerfoot, D. and Whitehead, D. (2000) 'Keeping all the balls in the air: FE and the masculine managerialist subject'. *Journal of Further and Higher Education* 24, 2, 184–99.

Kerry, T. and Tollitt-Evans, J. (1992) *Teaching in Further Education*. Oxford: Blackwell.

Kingston, P. (2003) 'The Third Way'. *Guardian Education (Further)*. 1 July, 46.

Kitchen, P. (1944) *From Learning to Earning*. London: Faber and Faber.

Knowles, M. (1980) *The Modern Practice of Adult Education: From pedagogy to andragogy*. Cambridge: Cambridge Book Company.

Knowles, M. (1985) *Andragogy in Action: Applying modern principles of adult learning*. San Francisco: Jossey Bass.

Laningan, E. (1994) 'The development of individual action planning. Unpublished MA dissertation for VET, Institute of Education, University of London.

Lau-Walker, T. (1995) 'Further education and GNVQs'. In L. Glover (ed.), *GNVQs into Practice: How was it for you?* London: Cassell.

Lave, J. (1993) 'The practice of learning'. In S. Chailklen and J. Lave (eds), *Understanding Practice*. Cambridge: Cambridge University Press.

Lave, J. and Wenger, E. (1994) *Situated Learning: Legitimate peripheral participation*. Cambridge: Cambridge University Press.

LCC (1903) *Report of the Technical Education Board*. London: London County Council.

Leathwood, C. (2000) 'Happy families? Pedagogy management and parental discourses of control in the incorporated college'. *Journal of Further and Higher Education* 24, 2, 163–81.

Le Grand, J. and Bartlett, W. (1993) *Quasi-Markets and Social Policy*, Basingstoke and London: Macmillan.

Lea, J., Hayes, D., Armitage, A., Lomas, L. and Markless, S. (2003) *Working in Post-Compulsory Education*. Maidenhead: Open University Press.

Leney, T., Lucas, N. and Taubman, D. (1998) *Learning Funding: The impact of FEFC funding: evidence from twelve FE colleges*. London: NATFHE.

Lipshitz, S. (1972) *Wastage among Craft Apprentice Students*. Brunel FE Monographs, No 4. London: Hutchinson.

Long, D. (1990) *Learner Managed Learning: The key to lifelong learning and development*. London: Kogan Page.

Longworth, N. and Davis, W. (1996) *Lifelong Learning*. London: Kogan Page.

LSC (2003) *Success for All – Implementing the framework for quality and success*. Learning and Skills Council Consultation Document Circular 03/01. Coventry.

— (2003a) *Plan Led Funding for Further Education*. Learning and Skills Council Consultation Document Circular 03/15. Coventry.

Lucas, N. (1996) 'Teacher Training Agency: Is there anyone there from further education?' *Journal of Further and Higher Education* 20, 1, 67–73.

— (1997) 'The applied route at age 14 and beyond – implications for initial teacher education' In A. Hudson and D. Lambert (eds), *Exploring Futures in Initial Teacher Education*. London: Institute of Education, University of London.

— (1999) 'Incorporated colleges: beyond the further education funding council's model'. In A. Green and N. Lucas (eds), *FE and Lifelong Learning: Realigning the*

Sector for the 21st Century. London: Institute of Education, University of London.
— (2000) 'Towards professionalism: teaching in further education'. In D. Gray, and C. Griffin, (eds), *Post-Compulsory Education and the New Millennium*. London: Jessica Kingsley.

Lucas, N. and Betts, D. (1996) 'The incorporated college: human resource development and human resource management: contradictions and options'. *Research In Post-Compulsory Education* 1, 3, 329–45.

Lucas, N. and Mace, J. (1999) 'Funding issues and social exclusion: reflections on the 'marketisation' of further education colleges'. In A. Hayton (ed.), *Tackling Disaffection and Social Exclusion*. London: Kogan Page.

Lucas, N., Cunningham, B., Poland, S. and Scott, I. (1996) *Partnership in Teacher Education for the FE Sector*. Post 16 Education Centre Working Paper 20. London: Institute of Education, University of London.

Lucas, N., McDonald, J. and Taubman, D. (1999) *Learning to Live with it: The impact of FEFC funding, further evidence from fourteen colleges*. London: NATFHE.

Lucas, N., Casey, H., Loo, S., McDonald, J., Grannakaki, M. and Young, M. (2004) *New Initial Teacher Education Programmes for Teachers of Literacy, Numeracy and ESOL: An exploratory study*. London: National Research and Development Centre for Adult Literacy and Numeracy.

Lumby, J. and Tomlinson. H. (2000) 'Principles speaking: managerialism and leadership in further education. *Research in Post-compulsory Education* 5, 2, 139–52.

Macadam, M. and Sutcliffe, J. (1996) *Still a Chance to Learn: A report on the impact of the Further and Higher Education Act (1992) on education for adults with learning difficulties*. Leicester: NIACE.

McClelland, K. (1990) 'The transmission of collective knowledge: apprenticeships in engineering and shipbuilding 1850–1914'. In P. Summerfield and E. Evans (eds), *Technical Education and the State since 1850*. Manchester: Manchester University Press.

McCullock, G. (1987) 'History and Policy: The politics of TVEI'. In D. Gleeson (ed.), *TVEI and the Secondary School: A critical appraisal*. Milton Keynes: Open University Press.

Macfarlane, E. (1993) *Education 16–19 in Transition*. London: Routledge.

McGavin, H. (1998) 'Cut salaries or lose jobs, lecturers told'. *TES* (*FE Focus*) 24 April.

McGinty, J. and Fish, J. (1993) *Further Education in the Market Place*. London: Routledge.

Mackey, J. (2003) 'Lifelong Learning Sector Skills Council'. Unpublished presentation given at the DfES Second Annual Teaching and Learning Conference, 4 November.

Mackney, P. (1998) 'Move on after the misery'. *TES* (*FE Focus*) 3 April.

McNair Report (1944) *Teachers and Youth Leaders*. Board of Education, London: HMSO.

Mahony, P. and Hextall, I. (2000) *Reconstructing Teaching: Standards, performance and accountability*. London: RoutledgeFalmer.

Mansfield, B. (1989) 'Competency and Standards'. In J. Burke (ed.), *Competency Based Education and Training*. London: Falmer.

— (1990) 'What is knowledge and understanding?'. In H. Black and A. Wolf (eds), *Knowledge and Competence: Current issues in training and education*. London: HMSO.

Matlay, H. (1997) 'The paradox of training in the small business sector of the British economy'. *Journal of Vocational Education and Training* 49, 4, 573– 91.

Maynard, E. (1995) 'What about male mature students? A comparison of men and women students'. *Journal of Access Education* 9, 2, 299–40.

Maynard, T. (1996) 'The limits of mentoring'. In R. Smith and J. Furlong (eds), *The Role of Higher Education in Initial Teacher Training*. London: Kogan Page.

Meagher, N. (1997) 'Classroom observation in academic and vocational courses post 16'. In T. Edwards, C. Fitz-Gibbon, F. Hardman, R. Haywood and N. Meagher (eds), *Separate But Equal? A Levels and GNVQs*. London: Routledge.

Millis, C. (1925) *Technical Education: Its development and aims*. London: Edward Arnold.

MoE (1946) *Further Education 1946–1947 Major Establishments (other than Arts)*. London: HMSO.

— (1956) *Technical Education*. White Paper. Ministry of Education. London: HMSO.

— (1957) *The Supply and Training of Teachers in Technical Colleges*. The Willis Jackson Report. London: HMSO.

— (1959) *15–18: A report of the Central Advisory Council for Education*. The Crowther Report. London: HMSO.

— (1961) *Better Opportunities in Technical Education*. Circ 1/61. London: HMSO.

Moser Report (1999) *Improving Literacy and Numeracy: A fresh start*. Sudbury: Department for Education and Employment.

Morris, E. (2001) 'Ask the bosses'. *Guardian Education*. 16 October, 39.

Mortimore, P. (1999) *Understanding Pedagogy and its Impact on Learning*.

London: Sage.

MSC (1981) *A New Training Initiative*. Sheffield: Manpower Services Commission.

— (1982) *Youth Task Group Report*. London: Manpower Services Commission.

Munby, H. and Russell, T. (1993) 'Reflective teacher education: technique or epistemology?' *Teaching and Teacher Education* 9, 4, 431–8.

Nash, I. (1999) 'Super-lecturer age dawns'. *TES* (*FE Focus*) 8 January, 31.

— (2003) 'An honest council for the people'. *TES* (*FE Focus*) 31 October, 1.

NATFHE (1994) *Training to Teach in Further Education*. London: National Association of Teachers in Further and Higher Education.

NEC (1991) *Flexistudy – Some Questions Answered*. Cambridge: National Extension College.

Newman, J. and Clarke, J. (1994) 'Going about our business? The managerialism of public services'. In J. Clarke, A. Cochrane and E. McLaughlin (eds), *Managing Social Policy*. London: Sage.

NIACE (1990) *NVQs. UDACE Development Paper*. National Institute of Adult and Community Education. Leicester: NIACE.

— (1998) *Realising the Learning Age: A response to the Government Green Paper*. Leicester: NIACE.

NTONC (1999) *An Employer's Guide to National Training Organisation*. Sheffield: NTO National Council.

— (1999a) *A New Era of Training for Britain*. Sheffield: NTO National Council.

Ofsted (1996) *Assessment of GNVQs in Schools 1995/6*. London: HMSO.

— (2003) *The Initial Training of Further Education Teachers: A survey*. HMI 1762. London: Ofsted.

Ollin, R. (1996) 'Learning from industry: human resource development and the quality of lecturing staff in further education'. *Quality Assurance in Education* 4, 4, 29–36.

Patrick, H., Bernbaum, G. and Reid, K. (1982) *The Structure and Process of Initial Teacher Education in Universities in England and Wales*. Leicester: Leicester School of Education.

Paul, R. (1990) *Open Learning and Open Management: Leadership and integrity in distance learning*. London: Kogan Page.

Payne, L. and Edwards, R. (1996) 'Impartial guidance in further education colleges'. *Adults Learning* 7, 7, 160–1.

Peeke, G. (1999) Unpublished report to QCA on standards for teaching and supporting learning in FE England and Wales.

Peeke, G. and Spencer, I. (1998) 'Standards and qualifications. Accreditation and qualifications framework'. Unpublished report to the Awarding Bodies Sub-Group of the FESDA, 15 September.

Pelican, J. (1992) *The Idea of the University*. New Haven: Yale University Press.

Perry, A. (1997) *A Pencil Instead. Why we need a new funding system for further education*. London: Lambeth College.

Perry, Lord E. (1930) *Education at the Crossroads*. London: Evans Brothers.

Perry, P. (1976) *The Evolution of British Manpower Policy*. London: BACIE.

Peters, A. (1967) *British Further Education*. London: Pergamon.

Peters, R. (1977) *Education and the Education of Teachers*. London: Routledge.

Polanyi, M. (1967) *The Tacit Dimension*. New York: Doubleday.

Pring, R. (1985) 'In defence of TVEI'. *Forum* 27, 3, 73–80.

— (1992) 'Standards and quality in education'. *British Journal of Education Studies*. 40, 1, 4–22.

— (1995) *Closing the Gap: Liberal education and vocational preparation*. London: Hodder and Stoughton.

— (1996) 'Just dessert'. In R. Smith and J. Furlong (eds), *The Role of Higher Education in Initial Teacher Training*. London: Kogan Page.

PwC (2003) 'Review of funding for ITT in the post 16 sector'. Draft report submitted to the Department for Education and Skills by PricewaterhouseCoopers. November.

QCA (1999) *Qualifications 16–19*. London: Qualifications and Curriculum Authority.

Randle, K. and Bradey, M. (1997) 'Managerialism and professionalism in the "Cinderella" service'. *Journal of Vocational Education and Training* 49, 1, 121–40.

Randle, K. and Bradey, M. (1998) 'Further education and new managerialism'. *Journal of Further and Higher Education* 1, 2, 229–39.

Reeves, F. (1995) *The Modernity of Further Education*. Bilston: Bilston Community College Press.

Renolds, D. (1999) 'Yes'. *Times Educational Supplement*. 13 August.

Richardson, V. (1992) 'The evolution of reflective teaching and teacher education'. In R. Cliff, R. Houstan and M. Pugach (eds) *Encouraging Reflective Practice in Education*. New York: Teachers College Press.

Richardson, W. (1939) *The Technical College: Its organisation and administration*. London: Oxford University Press.

Richardson, W., Woolhouse, J. and Finegold, D. (eds) (1993), *The Reform of Post 16 Education and Training in England and Wales*. Harlow: Longman.

Robson, J. (1998) 'A profession in crisis: status, culture and identity in the further education college'. *Journal of Vocational Education and Training* 50, 4, 585–607.

— (1999) 'Outsiders on the inside: a first person account of the research process in a further education college'. *Research in Post Compulsory Education* 41, 1, 75– 94.

Roderick, G. and Stephens, M. (1978) *Education and Industry in the Nineteenth Century*. London: Longman.

Roland, S. (1991) *The Adult Curriculum: Explorations in active learning*. Sheffield: Division of Education, Sheffield University.

Russell Report (1966) *The Supply and Training of Teachers for Further Education*. Department of Education and Science. London: HMSO.

Ryan, P. (1999) 'The embedding of apprenticeship in industrial relations: British engineering 1925–65'. In P. Ainley and H. Rainbow (eds), *Apprenticeship: Towards a new paradigm of learning*. London: Kogan Page.

Ryle, G. (1949) *The Concept of Mind*. London: Hutchinson.

Salis, E. (1992) 'Total quality management in further education'. In T. Simkins, L. Ellison and V. Garratt (eds), *Implementing Education Reform: The early lessons*. Harlow: Longman.

Savory, C., Hodgson, A. and Spours, K. (2003) 'The Advanced Certificate of Vocational Education: A general or vocational qualification? Broadening the Advanced Level Curriculum'. IOE/Nuffield Series No. 7. London: School of Lifelong Education and International Development, Institute of Education, University of London.

Schon, D. (1983) *The Reflective Practitioner. How professionals think in action*. New York: Basic Books.

— (1988) 'Coaching reflective teaching'. In P. Grimmett and G. Erickson (eds), *Reflection in Teacher Education*. New York: Teachers College Press.

Scott, C. (2001) 'Caseloading and the changing roles of lecturers and managers'. *Journal of Further and Higher Education* 25, 2, 241–8.

Scott, P. (1995) *A Tertiary System. Report for the Society of Education Officers*. Leeds: Leeds University.

Selby-Smith, C. (1970) *The Costs of Further Education*. Oxford: Pergamon Press.

Select Committee (1867/8) *Report on Provision for Giving Instruction in Theoretical and Applied Science to the Industrial Class*. London: HM Government.

Senker, P. (1992) *Industrial Training in a Cold Climate*. Aldershot: Avebury.

Sheldrake, J. and Vickerstaff, S. (1987) *The History of Industrial Training in Britain*. Aldershot: Avebury.

Sherlock, D. (2003) 'The lost three million'. *Talisman* (Newspaper of the Adult Learning Inspectorate) 18 April, 1.

Shulman, L. (1986) 'Those who understand: knowledge and growth in teaching'. *Educational Researcher* 59, 6, 4–12.

Simmons, J. (1999) 'Working in cross-college roles in further education'. *Journal of Vocational Education and Training* 51, 4, 239–53.

Simon, B. (1965) *The Politics of Educational Reform, 1920–1940*. London: Lawrence and Wishart.

— (1969) *The Two Nations and the Education System, 1780–1870*. London: Lawrence and Wishart.

— (1974) *Education and the Labour Movement 1870–1920*. London: Lawrence and Wishart.

Singleton, D. (2003) 'Measuring success'. *Talisman* (Newspaper of the Adult Learning Inspectorate) 18 April, 8–9.

Skipper, C. and Quantz, C. (1987) 'Changes in educational attitudes of education and arts students during four years at college'. *Journal of Teacher Education* 38, 3, 39–44.

Smithers, A. and Robinson, P. (1993) *Changing Colleges: Further education in the market place*. London: Council for Industry and Higher Education.

SOEID (1997) *Draft National Guidelines on Provision Leading to the Teaching Qualification (FE) and Related Professional Development*. Edinburgh: The Scottish Office and Industry Department.

Spours, K. (1995a) *The Strengths and Weaknesses of GNVQs: An analysis of a curriculum model and principles of design. Learning for the future*. Post 16 Education Centre Working Paper 3. London: Institute of Education, University of London.

— (1997) 'Student retention issues: factors affecting institutional capability'. In N. Lucas (ed.), *Policy and Management Issues for Incorporated Colleges*. Post 16 Education Centre Working Paper 21. London: Institute of Education, University of London.

Spours, K. and Hodgson, A. (1996) *Value Added and Raising Attainment: A formative approach. A resource pack for practitioners*. Poole: BP Educational Services.

Spours, K. and Lucas, N. (1996) *The Formation of a National Sector of Incorporated Colleges: Developments and contradictions*. Post 16 Education Centre Working Paper 19. London: Institute of Education, University of London.

Squires, G. (1999) *Teaching as a Professional Discipline*. London: Falmer.

Stoney, S. and Lines, A. (1987) *YTS: The impact on FE*. Windsor: NFER-Nelson.

Stringer, J. and Richardson, J. (1982) *Policy Stability and Policy Change: Industrial training 1964–1982*. Public Administration Bulletin 39, 22–39.

Summerfield, P. and Evans, E. (1990) *Technical Education and the State Since 1850*. Manchester: Manchester University Press.

Sutton, A. (1992) 'The reform of vocational education'. In T. Whiteside, A. Sutton and T. Everton, *16–19 Changes in Education and Training*. London: David Fulton.

Thompson, E. (1963) *The Making of the English Working Class*. Harmondsworth: Penguin.

Thompson, S. (1879) *Apprentice Schools in France*. London.

Tomlinson, J. (1996) *Inclusive Learning*. Coventry: Further Education Funding Council.

TTA (2003) *Standards for the Award of Qualified Teacher Status*. London: Teacher Training Agency.

UCET (1999) Minutes of UCET Post-16 Committee. Unpublished. London, 29 April.

— (1999b) Minutes of Meeting of University Council for the Education of Teachers, Post-16 Committee. Unpublished. London, February.

— (2000) Papers laid on the table – recorded in Minutes of meeting of Post-16 Committee. Unpublished. London, 18 February.

— (2003) Interim report of OFSTED survey inspection given to the Post-16 Committee. Unpublished. London, February.

— (2003a) Minutes of UCET Post-16 Committee. Unpublished. London, 16 May.

University of Wolverhampton (1998) 'Report of "Standards for Teachers in FE: Report on mapping exercise"'. Unpublished. Wolverhampton: University of Wolverhampton.

Unwin, L. (1993) 'Training Credits: The pilot doomed to succeed'. In W. Richardson, J. Woolhouse and D. Finegold (eds), *The Reform of Post 16 Education in England and Wales*. London: Longman.

— (1997) 'Reforming the work-based route: problems and potential for change'. In A. Hodgson and K. Spours (eds), *Dearing and Beyond: 14–19 qualifications, frameworks and systems*. London: Kogan Page.

UPDC (1999) Survey of Certificate of Education and PGCE programmes in the post compulsory sector. Unpublished research by Fred Fawbet on behalf of the Universities Professional Development Consortium. October.

Usher, R. and Edwards, R. (1994) *Post Modernism and Education*. London: Routledge.

Usher, R., Bryant, I. and Johnston, R. (1997) *Adult Education and the Post Modern Challenge*. London: Routledge.

Van Driel, J., Verloop, N., Werven, I. and Dekkers, H. (1997) 'Teachers' craft knowledge and curriculum innovation in higher engineering education'. *Higher Education* 34, 105–22.

Venables, E. (1967) *The Young Worker at College – A study of a local Tech*. London: Faber and Faber.

Venman, S. (1984) 'The perceived problems of Beginning Teachers'. *Review of*

Educational Research 54, 143–78.

Watkins, C. and Mortimore, P. (1999) 'Pedagogy: What do we know?' In P. Mortimore (ed.), *Understanding Pedagogy and its Impact on Learning.* London: Sage.

Watts, A. (1990) 'The role of guidance in educational change'. In A. Watts (ed.), *Guidance and Education Change.* Cambridge: CRAC/Hobson.

Wedell, K. (1993) *Special Educational Needs: The next 25 years.* London: National Commission on Education.

Wedemeyer, C. (1981) *Learning at the Back Door.* Madison, WI: University of Wisconsin Press.

Weiss, J.H. (1982) *The Making of Technological Man: The social origins of French engineering education.* Cambridge, MA: MIT Press.

Widen, M. and Grimmett, P. (1995) *Changing Times in Teacher Education: Restructuring or reconceptualisation.* London: Falmer.

Williams, E. (1998) 'Leaner and fitter?' *FE Now!* Issue 50. December, 8–9.

Williams, S. (1999) 'Policy tensions in vocational education and training for young people: The origins of GNVQs'. *Journal of Education Policy* 14, 2, 151–66.

Willis Jackson Report (1956) *The Supply and Training of Teachers for Technical Colleges.* Report of Special Committee, Ministry of Education. London: HMSO.

Wilmot, M. and McLean, M. (1994) 'Evaluating flexible learning: a case study'. *Journal of Further and Higher Education* 18, 3, 99–108.

Wolf, A. (1995) *Competency Based Assessment.* Buckingham: Open University Press.

Wyatt, L. (1995) 'GNVQs in health and social care'. In L. Glover (ed.), *GNVQs into Practice: How was it for you?* London: Cassell.

Young, M. (1998) *The Curriculum of the Future: From the new sociology of education to a critical theory of learning.* London: Falmer.

Young, M. and Lucas, N. (1999) 'Pedagogy and learning in further education: new contexts'. In P. Mortimore (ed.), *Understanding Pedagogy and its Impact on Learning.* London: Sage.

Young, M., Lucas, N., Sharp, G. and Cunningham, B. (1995) *Teacher Education for the Further Education Sector: Training the lecturer of the future.* Post 16 Education Centre report for Association of Colleges. London: Institute of Education, University of London.

Index